Children as Citizens

This book discusses how consultations with young children could signal a change of thinking about how children might influence policy and shape the development of a child-friendly state. While the consultations in this study were germane to political decisions, they took place as multi-modal dialogue with children in their educational settings. Framed by Australia's national early years learning framework which focuses on children's belonging and identity, the consultations saw unique partnerships formed among children, educators, families and policy officers, providing ways in which children's voices may be engaged in educational spaces throughout the world.

Using a qualitative case study approach, these consultations were documented through observations, interviews, artefact collection and document analyses, allowing the authors to construct a framework for engaging children as citizens that is transferable to a variety of settings.

Chapters provide:

- an insight into the various aspects involved in children's consultations from conceptualising and planning consultations with young children, to implementation and documentation, through to the uptake and consequence of children's messages;
- factors that contribute to the effectiveness of consultations, challenges that arise, and areas for improvement when engaging with children's voices;
- implications for children's participation as valued citizens and a framework for considering young children's voices in decision-making processes.

This book offers fresh ideas for working with young children in the decision-making process and will appeal to early childhood researchers, educators, policymakers and practitioners across various sectors, agencies and disciplines.

Pauline Harris is the Lillian de Lissa Chair, Early Childhood (Research) at the University of South Australia, in partnership with the South Australian Department for Education and Childhood Development, Australia.

Harry Manatakis is Principal Policy Adviser for the South Australian Department for Education and Child Development, Australia.

Routledge Research in Early Childhood Education

This series provides a platform for researchers to present their latest research and discuss key issues in Early Childhood Education.

Books in the series include:

Children as Citizens
Engaging with the child's voice in educational settings
Pauline Harris and Harry Manatakis

Children as Citizens

Engaging with the child's voice in educational settings

Pauline Harris and
Harry Manatakis

LONDON AND NEW YORK

First published 2013
by Routledge
2 Park Square, Milton Park, Abingdon, Oxon OX14 4RN

and by Routledge
711 Third Avenue, New York, NY 10017

Routledge is an imprint of the Taylor & Francis Group, an informa business

© 2013 P. Harris and H. Manatakis

The right of P. Harris and H. Manatakis to be identified as authors of
this work has been asserted by them in accordance with sections 77
and 78 of the Copyright, Designs and Patents Act 1988.

All rights reserved. No part of this book may be reprinted or
reproduced or utilised in any form or by any electronic, mechanical, or
other means, now known or hereafter invented, including photocopying
and recording, or in any information storage or retrieval system,
without permission in writing from the publishers.

Trademark notice: Product or corporate names may be trademarks or
registered trademarks, and are used only for identification and
explanation without intent to infringe.

British Library Cataloguing in Publication Data
A catalogue record for this book is available from the British Library

Library of Congress Cataloging in Publication Data
A catalogue record for this book has been requested.

ISBN: 978-0-415-71400-6 (hbk)
ISBN: 978-1-315-88302-1 (ebk)

Typeset in Galliard
by RefineCatch Limited, Bungay, Suffolk

As *children of the past* (and still young at heart),
we dedicate this book to the *children of the present*, from all nations, whom we
wish to empower to have an authentic voice
in their communities as valued and active citizens;
so that as adults they, too, might recognise
as competent human beings their own *children of the future* . . .
and in so doing, continue the cycle of nurture
that contributes to the richness of society we all share,
adult and child alike.
Pauline Harris and Harry Manatakis

I dedicate this book to my husband John Daley,
my constant love and best friend, with whom I gladly hold hands on our journey
of being and becoming who we are in this world.
Pauline Harris

A special thank you to my remarkable parents Maria and Artemis Manatakis
for the wonderful childhood memories
and my beautiful wife Sarah Jane for being such a lovely soul
and my source of inspiration –
together we, too, will create great memories with our children someday.
Harry Manatakis

Contents

Acknowledgements	viii
Introduction: the Children's Voices Project	ix
1 Engaging with children as valued active citizens	1
2 The inquiry into the Children's Voices Project	15
3 Planning to engage with children as active citizens	29
4 Children make their voices visible through visual arts in Limestone Town	47
5 Children see themselves in a new frame through photography in an Eyre and Western community	65
6 Children weave their desires into a shared vision for their Fleurieu community	81
7 Children express their views through music, drama and play in a Western Adelaide community	93
8 Authentically documenting children's messages	106
9 Reporting and uptake of children's messages	118
10 Final reflections on the Children's Voices Project	133
References	143
Index	148

Acknowledgements

We gratefully acknowledge the support of the following people and organisations who made this work possible:

The Lillian de Lissa Trust Fund of South Australia, who funded the investigation of the Children's Voices Project, on which this book is based.

Ms Miriam Daley (South Australian Department for Education and Child Development) and Ms Audra Cooper (previously of the South Australian Department of the Premier and Cabinet) for their drive and initiative with the statewide consultations with young children in the Children's Voices Project.

Ms Cathy Walsh and Mr John Daley for their research assistant support of the investigation of the Children's Voices Project.

Ms Kerryn Jones for her work and insights on the statewide consultations from an early years learning perspective and in the context of *Belonging, being and becoming: the early years learning framework for Australia* (DEEWR, 2009).

Dr Eleni Giannakis for her support in the production phase of this book.

Windmill Theatre for their participation in the consultations and the insights and talents that Windmill staff and other local experts in their craft brought to the consultations.

Educators who implemented and documented the statewide consultations with children in their early childhood sites.

And most importantly, children and families for their engagement in the consultations – their participation has provided us all with many rich insights that are a lasting legacy of this project.

Introduction

The Children's Voices Project

One cannot expect positive results from an educational or political action program which fails to respect the particular view of the world held by the people. Such a program constitutes cultural invasion, good intentions notwithstanding.

(Freire, 1983, p. 84)

More than one-off events, consultations with children are a way of being for children and adults alike. It is in this consultative space that the identity of and relationships with young children as valued active citizens are honoured and nurtured, and their political, cultural and intellectual legacy understood. This book makes a unique and very timely contribution to understanding the journey taken when genuinely engaging with young children in this space.

Framed by the notion of child as valued active citizen, and in the context of the United Nations Convention on the Rights of the Child (1989), UNICEF's Child-Friendly Cities model (UNICEF Innocenti Research Centre, 2001), this book provides a comprehensive account of the 'Children's Voices Project'. In this project, 350 three- to eight-year-old children (with a small number of nine- to twelve-year-olds) participated in their state government's community consultations across eleven diverse government regions in South Australia – a state in the southern central part of Australia, with a total land area of 983, 482 square kilometres and a population of over 1.6 million people. These consultations focused on what is important to children in their communities and what children wish for in their lives.

These consultations were more than listening to children. Accordingly, this book draws on the full scope of the Children's Voices Project to provide in-depth accounts of what it means to truly encounter the child – to give the child opportunity and provocation to express their views over time, to listen to the child with all our senses, and to document the meanings children convey in ways that are authentic and true to what children express. How we accurately and faithfully represent children's input in government reports and the like to progress to the next stage of decision-making, and how we track the uptake and impact of children's input – these are also integral to what it means to engage with children's voices and participation in democratic processes, and are examined

x Introduction: the Children's Voices Project

throughout this book, including case study accounts of the consultations at four early childhood sites.

We write for those not only in South Australia but further afield nationally and internationally, who share a commitment to children's voices and citizenship. This broad audience includes, of course, early childhood educators, researchers, policymakers and practitioners across various sectors, agencies and disciplines – and also has relevance for those engaging with older children and young people, and those whose work more indirectly relates to children and young people. Our aims are to:

- Develop insight into the processes involved in children's consultations from conceptualising and planning consultations with young children, to implementation and documentation, through to the uptake and consequence of children's messages.
- Examine factors that contribute to the effectiveness of such consultations, challenges that arise, and areas for improvement when engaging with children's voices.
- Explore implications for children's participation as valued citizens, and provide a framework relevant to those engaging with young (and indeed older) children as valued, active citizens.

Partnerships among researchers, policymakers and children, families and educators in the field at large, were central to these consultations, and indeed to acting upon children's citizenship and the building of a 'child-friendly' state. In this sense, consulting with children is not only about dialogue with children – but dialogue among all who are invited in the encounter. We describe how these partnerships were forged, and the roles and relationships of those involved in the children's consultations. This account fosters understanding that consulting with children is more than a one-off event – it involves sustained engagement over time, and what occurs before and after the consultations is as important as the consultations themselves.

In focusing on the voices of children as valued citizens, the book draws on Loris Malaguzzi's notion of the 'hundred languages of children'[1] and depicts multimodal processes for engaging children's voices, including music, dance, song, story-telling, drama, visual arts, photography as well as spoken and written words.

While this book is primarily about engaging with young children's voices, it includes the voices of all who were involved in the children's consultations and what this engagement meant to them. This book is co-authored by a senior early childhood academic and researcher, and a senior early childhood policy adviser, with voices of educators, children, families and other policy personnel heard in their own words throughout the book.

The book is organised into ten chapters:

Chapter 1, 'Engaging with children as valued active citizens', establishes the conceptual framework and principles that guided the Children's Voices Project across eleven diverse localities in South Australia. Principles are framed by a Freirean perspective of enacting children's citizenship, awakening children's awareness of themselves as citizens with others in their world and valuing their voice in dialogic encounters in and about their world (Freire, 1983). This chapter reviews literature on engaging children's voices and democratic participation in matters affecting their lives. Children's rights and responsibilities are explored in relation to the research literature as well as the UN Convention on the Rights of the Child and UNICEF's Child Friendly Cities framework. Principles of enacting children's valued citizenship are described in terms of dialogic encounter (Freire, 1983), related to what occurs when consulting with children and, as importantly, what happens afterwards in relation to genuine deliberation and considered uptake of children's contributions.

Chapter 2, 'The inquiry into the Children's Voices Project', provides an account of the case study approach used to inform reflexivity in and beyond the Children's Voices Project in terms of the efficacy and value of the consultations, and the development of processes and tools for future use. To these ends, the inquiry into the Children's Voices Project was conducted as a qualitative case study (Yin, 2009) – the case being the South Australian state jurisdiction, with four embedded site-based case studies. Consultations were conducted at the sites of children's services in eleven different government regions. The early childhood educators who implemented the consultations were experienced leaders in their field. This chapter provides profiles of each site and the demographic of its broader community, presenting a broad range of socio-economic, cultural and geographical circumstances. Data were gathered through observations, interviews, artefacts and document analysis, from their planning to their implementation, reporting and uptake. Each of these methods is described, as is the approach to emergent analysis and means for ensuring the study's trustworthiness.

Chapter 3, 'Planning to engage with children as active citizens', provides a detailed account of the planning of the consultations with young children, drawing on data from interviews, participant observations and document analyses. The chapter accounts for how the idea of the consultations began; how the planning took shape; who was involved; the literature that was drawn on; and the engagement of the early childhood field to assist in implementing the consultations as part of their curriculum work with children, framed by Australia's new *Early Years Learning Framework* (DEEWR, 2009). The collaborative approach to the consultations is described in terms of cross-agency collaboration and partnership engagement with early childhood educators and families at their children's services sites. The key questions shaping the consultations are identified, as are the strategies that were developed for engaging young children. An account of the induction package and workshop that were designed for educators implementing the consultations is provided.

xii Introduction: the Children's Voices Project

Chapter 4, 'Children make their voices visible through visual arts in Limestone Town', presents the first of the four site-based case studies included in this book. It describes the consultations in a kindergarten and rural care service in a small rural community, where children aged two to four years engaged through visual arts. Local artists interacted with educators and children to talk about their craft. The artists made their work physically and conceptually available to children, enriching children's oral and visual literacies through which they expressed what was important to them in their communities and what they wished for in their lives. This case study brings into clear focus the power of taking young children's minds seriously, showcasing their capacity for sustained attention and somewhat technical conversation about abstract ideas.

Chapter 5, 'Children see themselves in a new frame through photography in an Eyre and Western community', describes the implementation and documentation of children's consultations in a home learning partnership programme in a rural and remote community. Children were engaged in the consultations through photography and information technology. This case study tells a compelling story of empowerment that comes from recognising the competent child – and shifting preoccupation from *what* children are (e.g. developmentally delayed, disabled, impaired) to *who* children are. Accompanied by adults' scaffolding, the simple act of providing digital cameras to children – many of whom had never seen or used a camera before, some of whom had serious developmental delays and disabilities – gave rise to powerful stories of how these children exercised their citizenship through modes they know best – play and an inquiring mind.

Chapter 6, 'Children weave their desires into a shared vision for their Fleurieu community', describes the consultations in an out-of-school-hours care service in a regional locality, where children were engaged through drawing and painting. Cross-site and cross-age collaborations among older and younger children were key features of this engagement. Accompanied by ongoing dialogue and drafting of ideas, children painted images of what was important to them in their communities and future lives, onto calico squares. These squares were sewn together as a wall hanging. Children's expression of material themes was infused with their social themes – the social remaining constant even as the children's expression of their material desires shifted from day to day in this encounter. Particularly prominent were these children's sense of solidarity and wellbeing that came from being connected with others. Hence the value of the quilt that gave scope for both individual expression and a synthesis that found common ground and brought together children and their ideas.

Chapter 7, 'Children express their views through music, drama and play in a Western Adelaide community', explores the fourth and final site-based case study in this book. It provides an account of the consultations in a suburban children's centre and out-of-school-hours care. Music, movement, drama and exploratory and dramatic play were brought together to engage the children. The chapter describes how the children's usual space in their centre was transformed through simple means in this engagement, and the profound impact of this change on children's and educators' thinking and participation. Key themes emerging from this case study include how music, movement, drama and play empowered children to re-imagine their realities as they explored and expressed what was important to them in their lives. To the responsive observer and watchful listener, children revealed as much about what was important to them through the process of their dialogic, playful engagement as through the outcomes of what they actually said.

Chapter 8, 'Authentically documenting children's messages', provides an account of how educators documented children's voices in their sites and conveyed children's thematic interests and concerns to the state government's education and child development agency. The processes involved, and the considerations, struggles and challenges encountered in these documentation processes, are explored. How these challenges were met are described, addressing authenticity and the complexity of documenting and reporting children's views, expressed through multiple modes, for government agencies, from which key messages could be distilled to meaningfully inform policy directions. Examples of documentation from the book's four case studies are included in this chapter.

Chapter 9, 'Reporting and uptake of children's messages', examines the next vital step in the consultations with young children – how government personnel made sense of educators' reports to thematise and synthesise children's messages from 350 children across the state, and package this information as an official report to the Department of the Premier and Cabinet. This chapter provides an account of children's themes from the eleven regions that were involved in the consultations. Government's uptake of children's messages is examined in terms of the distillation of children's messages and the incorporation of these messages in a community engagement report. This chapter maps the key points in this report onto what children actually expressed in their consultations.

Chapter 10, 'Final reflections on the Children's Voices Project', marked the beginning of a journey on which South Australia as a society has embarked to engage with young children in dialogic encounter. In this final chapter, we reflect on what this journey has meant thus far across South Australia's diverse localities, from the moment of the inception of these consultations through to ongoing consequences. We include educators' re-framings of their thoughts and actions in consequence of implementing and documenting the consultations in their sites, and a senior policy adviser reflects. We reflect, too, on what it means to act on the unequivocal belief in young children's capacity to engage in dialogue with others about their world – dialogue framed as multi-modal co-construction between educator and child, endowed with meaning and consequence and infused with qualities, among others, of mutual trust and critical thinking. We provide a framework of principles for researchers, policymakers, educators and practitioners in other fields who share this journey of engaging with young children's voices and nurturing their valued, active citizenship.

Note

1. Loris Malaguzzi, founder of the Reggio Emilia philosophy, wrote a poem called *The hundred languages of children*. In the first part of the poem, he celebrates the many different ways children express themselves; and in the second part, laments schools taking most of these languages away from children. The poem can be found at: http://www.thewonderoflearning.com/history/?lang=en_GB (retrieved 18 May 2012).

Chapter 1

Engaging with children as valued active citizens

No one is born fully-formed: it is through self-experience in the world that we become what we are.

Paulo Freire (1921–97)

Children are citizens of today and bearers of human rights. They are social actors, agents in their own lives, with the right among others to be active participants in decisions that affect their lives (United Nations Convention on the Rights of the Child, 1989). But what do these assertions mean for how children learn to engage as valued active citizens, and for how early childhood educators view and engage with the child?

These questions comprise the key focus throughout this book, which reports on a study of consultations with young children (three- to eight-year-olds, with a small number of older children aged nine to twelve also included), about their views of their local communities to inform a government's state strategic plan. These consultations were conducted in partnership with experienced early childhood educators in their education and care settings. Children's and educators' documented experiences of these consultations provide valuable insights into engaging with the child as social actor, active participant – as valued citizen.

Child as citizen

In a democratic society, ability to have a voice and participate in influencing public policy and social determinants within the community, are central tenets of citizenship. These central tenets hold true when their associated practices are authentic, non-tokenistic in nature and able to influence change in a way that is reflective of a broad representation of society's views.

However, in Australia – the national context of this book's project – the Child Right's NGO Report stated that 'mechanisms for involving children in decision-making . . . are poor . . . Australia does not follow best practice for finding out and incorporating the views of children' (*Listen to Children 2011 Child Right's NGO Report* Australia Executive Summary, p. 3).

2 Engaging with children as valued active citizens

In more global terms, the Committee on the Rights of the Child's General Comment No. 7 (2006) noted insufficient attention given to young children as rights holders, and reaffirmed 'that the Convention on the Rights of the Child is to be applied holistically in early childhood, taking account of the principle of the universality, indivisibility and interdependence of all human rights' (UN Committee on the Rights of the Child, 2006, p. 62). In this reaffirmation, the Committee sought 'recognition of young children as social actors from the beginning of life' (UN Committee on the Rights of the Child, 2006, p. 61).

Acknowledging young children as social actors brings our work into the realm of the new sociology of childhood (Noble-Carr, 2006). Children are viewed as competent human beings, key informants and experts on their own lives with views they express with wisdom and insight – indeed, our best source of advice for matters affecting them (Mac Naughton *et al.*, 2008). Recognising children this way shapes the relationships we develop with young children and how we engage with them as citizens not only on public matters in the civic sphere, but on matters in children's everyday lives and settings.

Such engagement, however, has not been without its obstacles and counter-arguments against engaging children's voices (Hallett and Prout, 2003). While some would question young children's capacity for such engagement, and others may doubt the age appropriateness of such action, there are still others who question adults' right to search for children's points of view (Eide and Winder, 2005, cited in Rhedding-Jones *et al.*, 2008).

It has been further noted that perceived benefits of engaging with children's voices are usually defined by adults and not children (Bishop, 2009). These benefits include opportunities for experiencing and learning about participation and inclusion in democratic and day-to-day processes; valuing and validating children's views, developing children's competencies for participation, contributing to decision-making processes and influencing change (Wise, 2009). However, as Bishop (2008) argues, there is need to spend more time understanding what constitutes benefit from children's (and young people's) perspectives.

A key conclusion of the 2012 'Child in the City' Conference in Zagreb was the reminder that children's rights in their entirety are human rights, and noted 'that the right to participate sometimes dominates the agenda, with disproportionate time and effort expended on developing representative structures and bodies for children's "voices" to be heard'. We had two observations about this:

A. That working with relatively well-off children in forums of young democracy should not take priority over working for all children's most basic rights to safety, shelter, food, love and the freedom to play.

B. Participation work should avoid aping adult institutions. Children should rather be enabled to participate fully in their lives as children, communicating and exercising their own agency through their own mediums of play and movement as much as being listened to when they speak.[1]

These challenges create opportunities for re-framing our thinking and transforming our practices – as policymakers and educators found themselves doing in engaging with children's voices as reported in this book. In this space, we do not view children's basic rights and freedom to play to be contradictory with children's right to be heard in decisions that affect their lives. But we do pay heed to the need for balance among children's rights – and the importance of play in young children's lives.

These challenges highlight the complexity of children's participation, rights and citizenship. We need to learn from this complexity so that we might improve our understanding and practice in relation to more fully realising children's rights and citizenship, as comprehensively documented across a range of approaches in diverse contexts around the world (Percy-Smith and Thomas, 2009).

The tension that resides in the challenges we've identified here, it seems, concerns children's right to be children. Part of being children, of course, is being human, and recognising young children's citizenship in the here-and-now. In approaching matters related to young citizenship – such as engaging with young children in consultations to inform decisions affecting their lives – we need to be mindful of how children express their citizenship in ways that are part and parcel of how they act in and with their world. We return to this dilemma to explore it further later in the chapter.

Before we do further explore how we engage with young children as citizens, we need some clarity about what citizenship actually means in a democratic society, which is the political context of this book. Definitions of citizenship abound, including the legal sense of being citizens of one's country of birth, with all the rights that go with that particular constitutionally defined, politically demarcated and geographically bound citizenship. A legal recognition of citizenship alone, however, does not equate to meaningful or valued citizenship – it does not capture the deeper implications of what it means to be a citizen, such as what it means to belong and be included because one is a citizen, and the relationship between citizenship and rights, citizenship and wellbeing (Ben-Arieh and Boyer, 2005).

A strictly legal definition of citizenship might rest comfortably with the notion of children as citizens from birth for those holding traditional views of early childhood (Alderson *et al.*, 2005). However, such a definition does not capture the essence of what it means for a young child or infant to be an *active citizen* – defined by Isen and Turner (cited in Phillips, 2011, p. 784) as 'being a social agent expressing opinions, making decisions, and enacting social actions as an expression of civic responsibility'.

Inherent in the notion of child as active citizen from birth is recognition of the child as competent: 'children can be seen as citizens, from their earliest years, because they are able to express ideas and wants and to contribute to decision-making that affects them' (Nutbrown and Clough, 2009, p. 196).

However, is active citizenship simply expressing civic responsibility by expressing ideas, opinions and wants that contribute to pertinent decision-making processes? There are those who argue from a Freirean perspective that active democratic

4 Engaging with children as valued active citizens

citizenship involves participating in the world in order to transform it, with a sense of social justice and self-awareness of one's presence in the world in relation to others. As Brett (2007, p.1) has argued:

> Discourses centring around concepts such as 'participation', 'empowerment' and 'active democratic citizenship' are widely used in education but can easily be misappropriated by the New Right – and/or indeed 'New Labour' (cf. Ledwith, 1997). Participation with an emphasis upon duty, and without political drivers, can collapse into an unproblematic conception of active citizenship as volunteering.

This note of caution is a timely reminder that children's engagement with civic decision-making processes – a practice often seen to be the hallmark of children's active citizenship – can only be significant if conditions are in place that endow children's participation with authenticity, meaning and consequence – conditions that at the same time foster children's learning about what it means to be valued active citizens.

Translating findings into policy or practice is a major aspiration of engaging with children as active citizens. There have been indications, however, that while there is clear enthusiasm for children's participation, evidence of change as a consequence of children's participation is less apparent (Fitzgerald and Graham, 2009). That being the case, there is a need to interrogate if and how children's participation is working in children's favour, and to understand the implications for children's sense of participation and citizenship when their views are sought but not taken up in any substantial way that makes a difference to their lives (Dockett, 2009; Wise, 2009).

Nurturing children's active citizenship

As Freire (1983, p. 72) has written, people – adults and children alike – are 'beings in the process of becoming – unfinished, uncompleted beings in and with a likewise unfinished reality'. It is through experience in the world that we become who we are. It follows, then, that what children experience as citizens shapes who they are and who they become as citizens. Therein lie significant implications for how we engage and interact with children in our early childhood settings. As Taylor *et al.* (2008, p. 196) have maintained, citizenship is 'learned and practiced in the contexts of family, school and community social participation . . . and it is likely to be through social relationships and processes in society that children come to understand citizenship'.

Therefore, as Percy-Smith (2010, p. 109) has provocatively argued, opportunities need to be provided for young children

> to participate more fully in everyday community settings – home, school and neighbourhood – through the actions, choices, relationships and contributions

Engaging with children as valued active citizens 5

they make, rather than being preoccupied with participation in political and public decision-making processes in organisations and systems which are removed from young people's everyday lives.

Returning to our earlier dilemma of balancing listening to children with their rights to play and exercise agency in their everyday worlds, we now explore conditions that nurture young children's sense and mobilisation of self as active citizens in their everyday contexts, and endow their participation with authenticity, meaning and consequence. The practice often referred to as 'consulting with children' to inform decision-making in any authentic, meaningful and consequential way requires dialogue in the Freirean sense of the word – a conversation space in which children and adults come together in dialogue in and about the world. As Freire (1983, p. 124) compellingly wrote:

> Some may think that to affirm dialogue – the encounter of people in the world in order to transform the world – is naïvely and subjectively idealistic. There is nothing, however, more real or concrete than people in the world and with the world, than humans with other humans.

Such dialogue involves an awakening of participants' consciousness of their presence in the world – an awakening that Freire (1983) referred to as conscientisation that he further explained:

> A humanising education is the path through which men and women can become conscious about their presence in the world. The way they act and think when they develop all of their capacities, taking into consideration their needs, but also the needs and aspirations of others.'
> (Freire and Frei Betto, 1985, pp. 14–15)

Such encounter provides opportunity to explore what it is to be a child in the world and what it means for a child to be an active citizen (Sommer, Samuelsson and Hundeide, 2010) – and more, what it means, as this book explores in chapters to come, to be educators and policymakers engaging with children's voices and participation in a democratic society.

Such encounter also affords opportunity for children to reflect on and live their lives from what Coady (2008, p. 12) has called the inside:

> Humans of whatever age need to live their lives from the inside according to their understandings of what makes life valuable, and be able to use the resources of their culture to assess these values in the light of whatever information and examples and arguments their culture can provide . . . Even very young children are in the same process of learning and of evaluating their beliefs about what makes life worthwhile, even while they are very dependent on their families and others around them for input and guidance.

6 Engaging with children as valued active citizens

Well might we consider, then, examples we wish to set young children about what it means to be an active citizen. We call on Freire's notion (1983) of the dialogic encounter to frame children's participation as active citizens – that is, dialogue between people in, with and about their world, giving rise to the identification of participant's thematic concerns or interests.

Posing problems or key questions form the basis of such encounter (Freire, 1983). Problem-posing questions interrogate the kind of society we live in, the kind of society and world we want in our future lives, and the actions we can take to effect change and make a difference in the world in which we live (Brett, 2007). It is through such provocation that participants may come to see the world not as a given static reality, but as realities filled with possibility and in the process of transformation. Seeing the world thus is a necessary condition of participants feeling empowered to summon their agency as active citizens to effect and influence change that they seek in their world (Friere, 1983).

In his own work, Freire (1983) was of the firm conviction that every human being is capable of critically engaging in a dialogical encounter with others. He did not qualify this assertion in terms of preconceived limits related to age, ability, language, ethnicity, social standing, political position, or other such factors. In turn, then, we are compelled to ask, what does this unequivocal belief in the capacity of human beings mean for how we engage with young children as valued, active citizens in and about their world?

A number of principles arise in response to this question in early childhood education contexts. One such principle is creating space for authentic dialogue between child and educator in the world and about the world (Freire, 1983). Such dialogue creates a relational context founded on mutual respect between child and educator, and is framed by what is meaningful from a child's perspective. In the context of children's consultations, this respect extends to deferring to children's desire not to participate.

Relationship is key to developing shared understanding and co-constructing the dialogic encounter among participants in and about their world. Freire (1983) has described qualities that infuse relationships in such encounter. One such quality is faith in people. In the context of children's consultations, there needs to be faith in children, in educators, and in those who are invested with the authority to act on the strength of what emerges from the encounter. Another quality is humility, which in children's consultations means seeing the competence of children as key informants about what concerns or interests them in their world. Freire (1983) speaks, too, of love in the dialogic encounter – love for the world and our fellow humans. Mutual trust, too, is essential – in children's consultations, this trust is a matter between child and educator that the consultations will be worthwhile, responsive to children's involvement, transparent in the consultations' purpose, and accountable in reporting and uptake. Hope is another key quality in dialogic encounters and to framing children's consultations as such – its opposite, hopelessness, only defeats the

Engaging with children as valued active citizens 7

purpose of asking children to inform change, and perpetuates a sense of negativity about such participation, as previously discussed in this chapter.

Framing children's consultations as dialogic encounter between young children and educators (or other adults) breaks down the dichotomy between child and educator by being framed as a co-constructed exploration of child-generated themes of relevance and interest to children in their world – thereby engaging children's participation while developing children's competencies for their participation. Co-construction is important for what is seen to be a key challenge in children's participation – that is, balancing young children's agency with their dependency in ways that minimise adult influences on what children say and do (Dockett, 2009; Harcourt, 2009; Sorin, 2009). Thus educators scaffold the child's engagement in his or her zone of proximal development (Vygotsky, 1978).

Essential to the dialogic encounter is opportunity for children to give voice to their perspectives in ways they can best express themselves. Such encounter is inclusive of all the modes through which children express themselves and project themselves onto their world – what indeed Malaguzzi[2] referred to as the 'hundred languages of children', including music, dance, song, story-telling, drama, visual arts, photography as well as spoken and written words. Most of all, there is play – for play, after all, is children's work and approach to thought and action in and about their world. Play provides a space where 'a child acts beyond his actual age, his daily behavior; in play it is as though he were a head taller than himself' (Vygotsky, 1978, p. 102). Play, then, is a conducive mode for children enacting their citizenship and expressing their voice and point of view.

Actively listening to the child is integral to the dialogic encounter. To actively listen is to engage with all one's senses and with the modes children have at their disposal. The highly regarded and effective mosaic approach, developed by Clark and Moss (2011), provides one means for multi-modal engagement with children's voices (see also Clark *et al.*, 2005; Smith *et al.*, 2000; Stephenson, 2009). Any such approach has the potential to yield rich accounts of what matters to children in ways that are authentic and true to what children express as valued citizens participating in democratic processes.

Such dialogue, too, makes real the valuing and release of the child's agency. In this context, we might well ask, if children are seen to be agents, what are they agents of? From a psychological or sociocultural perspective, we might say children are active agents of learning and constructing meaning. From a sociological point of view, we might define agency in terms of being social actors expressing needs, wants and desires. However, these perspectives do not capture what it means for a child to exercise agency as a citizen. To appreciate such agency, we need to move beyond seeing children as subjects of concern to subjects *with* concerns (Prout, 2000) or, we would say in this context, citizens with concerns.

In the context of children's citizenship, we view children as agents of meaning, of action, of change. Indeed, as a citizenship specialist teacher recently explained,

8 Engaging with children as valued active citizens

the concept of agency as it is understood not only by adults but by children and young people themselves

> can be developed by examining issues which students see as significant to their community (local, national and international) and then initiating action to influence these events. Thus the student, as an agent of change, develops the skills of political literacy as well as understanding of the significance of the institutions involved in this process.
>
> (Lawson, 2005, p. 14)

Using a dialogic encounter to examine issues and take action relies on using and transforming structures that support and sustain meaningful conversations. Appropriate structures are those that deepen the exploration of meaning in this dialogic space through the spoken word and other multiple modes that children have at their disposal. Engaging with young children as valued active citizens necessitates a preparedness to create space to listen to their views; and requires the provision of adequate time to explore issues, safe and nurturing environments, a true willingness to listen to each child, and an intention to take action.

Listening to each child in a group setting is a significant challenge, and if we under-estimate this challenge, we run the risk of privileging some children's voices while silencing others – especially children whose home languages may be ones other than those of the dominant discourses, or newly arrived immigrant and refugee children, or children with perceived language or developmental issues. As Rhedding-Jones *et al.* (2008, p. 48) also have argued in consequence of such privileging, learning about citizenship becomes 'an uneven affair, empowering some children and disempowering "others"'.

Also essential to the dialogic encounter in which we consult with children is authentic documentation of children's words and the thematic concerns they represent. This means stepping into children's shoes and understanding the world from their point of view – the perceptions children hold and what is of concern and interest to them, which comprise their 'thematic universe' (Freire, 1983, p. 86). Understanding children's thematic concerns means that:

> We must learn who the children are, and not focus on what we assume them to be – at risk, learning disabled, behavior disordered, etc. This means developing relationships with students and understanding their political, cultural and intellectual legacy.
>
> (Delpit, 2003, p. 19)

Principles of enacting children's valued citizenship extend to what happens in relation to genuine deliberation and considered uptake of children's contributions after they have engaged in dialogic consultations. Giving children a voice in such encounters does not in and of itself represent meaningful participation. As previously discussed in this chapter, transparency and accountability are

Engaging with children as valued active citizens 9

fundamental to building trust and promoting children's continued participation (Fitzgerald and Graham, 2009; Moore *et al.*, 2009). It is not sufficient for children to be listened to if their views are not taken seriously and if action does not follow as a result. Action does not always require concurrence with children's views – however, a respectful explanation of why children's views are unable to be followed through, or followed through in modified ways, in itself represents action founded on due acknowledgment of the value of children's contributions and place as citizens.

The South Australian Children's Voices Project

Principles described in this chapter for engaging with children as valued, active citizens bring us to the work at hand – the Children's Voices Project that involved dialogic consultations with young children about their local communities across the state of South Australia.

The broader national context for this work may be understood in terms of Australia's National Early Childhood Development Strategy launched in 2009 by the Council of Australian Governments, a peak intergovernmental forum bringing together federal, state and local government agencies. This strategy is framed by a vision that 'all children have the best start in life to create a better future for themselves and for the nation' (COAG, 2009, p. 13). Underscoring this vision is the simple but highly significant recognition that:

> Children are important. They bring their own value and influence to the world, as well as being shaped by the world around them . . . Children are also important for their future contribution to society, as the next generation of leaders, workers, parents, consumers and members of communities . . . in a global society.
>
> (COAG, 2009, p. 7)

Framed by a similar vision, the government of South Australia – a state in the southern central part of Australia with a total land area of 983,482 square kilometres and a population of over 1.6 million people – launched its review of its State Strategic Plan. This was a plan with measurable targets, visions and goals developed through extensive community consultation and guiding the whole community inclusive of individuals, community organisations, governments and businesses – including consulting with 350 young children (three- to eight-year-olds, with a small number of nine- to twelve-year-olds) across eleven diverse regions.

In this space, children engaged in consultations about their local communities – a matter not removed from their day-to-day lives and done in children's every-day early childhood education and care settings. Children's educators, involved in the planning, implementation and reporting of the consultations, framed the consultations in terms of Australia's national early childhood framework,

10 Engaging with children as valued active citizens

Belonging, being and becoming: an early years framework for Australia (DEEWR, 2009) – hereafter referred to as EYLF.

With an appreciation of what is currently important to children, what children wish for in their future lives, and children's sense of place and identity, these consultations resonated with EYLF that states:

> Experiences of relationships and participation in communities contribute to children's belonging, being and becoming. From birth, children experience living and learning with others in a range of communities. These might include families, local communities or early childhood settings. Having a positive sense of identity and experiencing respectful, responsive relationships strengthen children's interest and skills in being and becoming active contributors to their world.
>
> (DEEWR, 2009, p. 25)

The 'three Bs' of this curriculum framework – children's belonging, being and becoming – were integral to the framing of the consultations, in terms of children being citizens in the here and now; continuing to grow as citizens in their future lives; and their sense of belonging as active citizens.

The Children's Voices Project further linked to the following outcomes from EYLF:

- Outcome 1: 'Children feel safe, secure and supported. This is evident . . . when children openly express their feelings and ideas in their interactions with others . . . [and] respond to ideas and suggestions from others' (DEEWR, 2009, p. 21).
- Outcome 2: 'Children develop a sense of belonging to groups and communities and an understanding of the reciprocal rights and responsibilities necessary for active community participation. This is evident . . . when children express an opinion in matters that affect them' (DEEWR, 2009, p. 26).
- Outcome 5: 'Children are effective communicators, children interact verbally and non-verbally with others for a range of purposes, children engage in enjoyable interactions using verbal and non-verbal language' (DEEWR, 2009, p. 40).

These links to EYLF were to become part of ongoing professional development for educators facilitating the children's consultations, in terms of engaging children's voices and acknowledging and nurturing their place as valued citizens.

In order to base these statewide consultations on strong partnerships between the fields of early childhood research, policy and practice, South Australia's Department of the Premier and Cabinet (DPC) and the Department of Education and Children's Services (DECS) came together with the book's first author (Pauline Harris) as the de Lissa Chair in Early Childhood Research, and early childhood educators to plan and implement the consultations in children's services. Plans also were made for Professor Harris to investigate the consultations as they were conducted, to examine what worked well and what could be improved, and to develop a set of tools and resources for future use.

These consultations positioned children as active citizens whose views must be respected, as asserted in the *UN Convention on the Rights of the Child* (United Nations, 1989) and ratified by Australia in 1991 in recognition that children's rights are part and parcel of human rights:

> Article 3 (Best interests of the child): The best interests of children must be the primary concern in making decisions that may affect them. All adults should do what is best for children. When adults make decisions, they should think about how their decisions will affect children. This particularly applies to budget, policy and law-makers.
>
> Article 12 (Respect for the views of the child): When adults are making decisions that affect children, children have the right to say what they think should happen and have their opinions taken into account.[3]

In the spirit of respecting and upholding these rights in South Australia, the South Australian government in partnership with local government and community organisation partners committed to and has been working actively towards a 'Child Friendly SA' since late 2009. In committing to becoming 'child friendly', South Australia has been the first Australian state to make such an undertaking at a statewide level.

The 'Child Friendly SA' strategy expands on the UNICEF concept of 'child friendly cities' (UNICEF Innocenti Research Centre, 2001) that has been adopted in many cities throughout the world. Under the UNICEF framework, a Child Friendly City is committed to the fullest implementation of the Convention on the Rights of the Child. As such, a Child Friendly City guarantees among other rights the right of every young citizen to:

- Influence decisions about their city
- Express their opinion on the city they want
- Participate in family, community and social life
- Be an equal citizen of their city with access to every service, regardless of ethnic origin, religion, income, gender or disability.[4]

The South Australian approach has been a more ambitious undertaking in that it is based on a network of child friendly communities and cities linking together to realise a statewide child friendly vision. South Australia's approach to 'child friendly cities' recognises the importance of considering children's wellbeing, participation and voice in all policy development.[5]

Stages in the Children's Voices Project

Framing the consultations with young children as authentic dialogic encounters required careful deliberation before, during and after their implementation. Clearly, consulting with children is more than a one-off event – it involves sustained engagement over time, and what occurs before and after the consultations is as important as the consultations themselves. Six key stages unfolded, as outlined in Figure 1.1. We do not see these stages in a prescriptive or lock-step way, and the reality was that we moved recursively across stages. However, a schematic overview of these stages alerts us to the equal importance of what happens before, during and after consultations; and provides a coherent framework for organising the remainder of this book.

To summarise the enactment of these stages in the Children's Voices Project, consultations with South Australia's young children began with the initial planning and preparing of the consultations to ensure the consultations were

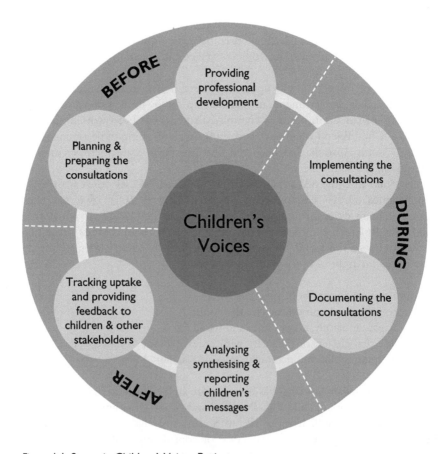

Figure 1.1 Stages in Children's Voices Project

Engaging with children as valued active citizens 13

adequately resourced in terms of material, time and people support, effective for all concerned stakeholders, and appropriate for the children who were to engage in the consultations.

This initial planning was followed by a professional development workshop to ensure all who were facilitating the consultations were supported and had opportunities to jointly explore principles and strategies for consulting with children and opportunities to tailor approaches to their particular children and contexts. These first two stages of planning the consultations are described in detail in Chapter 3.

The third key stage in engaging with children's voices is implementation, involving sustained engagement over time. Implementation of the Children's Voices Project is also introduced in Chapter 3 and explored in detail through four case studies in Chapters 4 to 7. The multi-modal nature of how the consultations were implemented in each early childhood site honoured Article 13 of the United Nations Convention on the Rights of the Child:

> The child shall have the right to freedom of expression; this right shall include freedom to seek, receive and impart information and ideas of all kinds, regardless of frontiers, orally, in writing or in print, in the form of art, or through any other media of the child's choice.[6]

As a key component of the consultations, documentation was an ongoing process throughout. Documentation served as a means for collective professional development and reflection among those involved in the consultations and for those looking on as possible future collaborators. Equally, documentation captured children's views to inform community planning. Approaches taken to documentation for the Children's Voices Project are described in Chapter 8, including examples of documentation in our four case studies.

The final two stages in the Children's Voices Project involved analysing, synthesising and reporting children's messages in ways that were authentic and true to children's meanings, while speaking to an official audience; and tracking uptake and consequence of children's messages and providing feedback to children and other stakeholders of this uptake. An account of these final two crucial stages is provided in Chapter 9, before bringing together key themes and re-framings in Chapter 10.

Before proceeding to the chapters that describe what occurred during these six stages of the Children's Voices Project, the following chapter explains how the inquiry into the Children's Voices Project was conducted to form the research basis of this book.

Notes

1. Conclusions of the *6th Child in the City Conference*, Zagreb, Croatia, 26–28 September 2012. http://www.childinthecity.com/Conclusion-Childrens-rights/page/8430/ (retrieved 24 October 2012).

14 Engaging with children as valued active citizens

2. Loris Malaguzzi, founder of the Reggio Emilia philosophy, wrote a poem called *The hundred languages of children*. In the first part of the poem, he celebrates the many different ways children express themselves and in the second part, laments schools taking most of these languages away from children. The poem can be found at http://www.thewonderoflearning.com/history/?lang=en_GB (retrieved 18 May 2012).
3. From *United Nations Convention on the Rights of the Child* (1989). http://www2.ohchr.org/english/law/crc.htm (retrieved 23 February 2012).
4. From UNICEF Innocenti Research Centre (2001) Child friendly cities. http://www.childfriendlycities.org/ (retrieved 23 February 2012).
5. For readers wishing to explore further the South Australian early childhood and care context and innovative practices in early childhood development, it is worth mentioning that as of October 2011 the Department of Education and Children's Services has brought together education and care with health and child welfare and safety as a realignment of key services for children, young people and their families, and the department since has been renamed the Department for Education and Child Development (DECD).
6. From *United Nations Convention on the Rights of the Child* (1989). http://www2.ohchr.org/english/law/crc.htm (retrieved 23 February 2012).

Chapter 2

The inquiry into the Children's Voices Project

A case study is an empirical inquiry that investigates a contemporary phenomenon in depth and within its real-life context.

(Yin, 2009, p. 18)

An inquiry into the Children's Voices Project as it was being conducted was developed to investigate and reflect upon the value and efficacy of engaging with the voices of children as valued, active citizens. The need for such reflection has been underscored by others who engage with children's participation – providing occasion for self-informing reflexivity that allows us to modify and learn from the processes in which we engage with children (Bishop, 2009; Moore *et al.*, 2009).

More specifically, the inquiry into the Children's Voices Project provided a means for investigating and reflecting upon:

- What the assertion of children as valued, active citizens means for how government agencies, in collaboration with early childhood educators and professionals, effectively engage with young children to inform their policy directions and decisions.
- How children and educators engage in consultations that are framed as dialogic encounters in and about their world.
- The consequences of this engagement for decision-making processes; for how children learn to engage as active citizens; and for how early childhood educators view and engage with the child.
- The development and use of effective tools and processes for further engagement with children as valued active citizens for other purposes in other contexts.

These consultations were examined and documented throughout their planning, professional development, implementation, documentation, reporting and uptake stages (that were described in Chapter 1 and shown in Figure 1.1). The investigation of the consultations was conducted as a qualitative case study (Yin, 2009), in which the bounded case was the state jurisdiction of South Australia

16 Inquiry into the Children's Voices Project

and contained four embedded site-based case studies. This chapter describes the conduct of this study that forms the research basis of this book.

Participants in the consultations

Among the 350 children who took part in the consultations in eleven early childhood sites across eleven different government regions in the state, 26 per cent of these children were Aboriginal children; approximately 20 per cent were children with additional needs; and 20 per cent of the children lived in rural, remote or isolated communities.

Care was taken to ensure children understood how and why they were being invited to take part in these consultations. In each site, children's parents or legal guardians were given an information sheet about the project and a written consent form. Children participated on a voluntary basis. Their identities were kept anonymous and their right to withdraw at any time without penalty was honoured.

After the consultations were finished, ethical considerations extended to providing feedback to children, in terms of explaining to children what would happen after their participation in the consultations, how their views have been important, and sharing what other children expressed. This feedback was valued in terms of recognising, acknowledging and validating children's contributions, thereby enhancing their sense of self-worth, place and community.

The children's early childhood educators were also key participants, who facilitated the consultations in their early childhood sites, in partnership with children's families. Together, these educators worked in a range of early childhood education and care services, as well as with some children in their family homes. Educators had both an established relationship with the children participating in the consultations and the expertise to explore children's views of their local communities in terms of Australia's learning framework, *Belonging, being and becoming: the early years learning framework for Australia* (DEEWR, 2009).

A lead educator in DECS provided professional development support across the services for linking the consultations to this national early childhood framework. Educators also engaged with local residents in their communities, who shared their creative and expressive arts to foster and deepen children's multi-modal engagement in the consultations – children's voices, after all, are not just verbal.

Senior directorial staff of DECS and the South Australian Department for Premier and Cabinet (hereafter DPC) were also key participants in this project. They championed the importance of children's consultations and ensured children's views were translated into action and valued in subsequent decision-making and policy.

The Children's Voices Project was co-ordinated by the book's second author (Manatakis), a senior policy adviser in DECS, who also provided relevant policy advice. Harris (this book's first author) advised on guiding principles for framing, implementing, documenting, analysing and interpreting the consultations in the Children's Voices Project; and conducted the case study inquiry into this project.

Sites where the consultations were conducted

Each site was chosen on the grounds of its strong early childhood education experience and leadership, and in light of achieving a balanced demographic coverage and inclusion of various service types across the eleven sites. Consequently, the selected sites ranged across urban, suburban, outer metropolitan, rural and remote localities; encompassed high, middle and low socio-economic circumstances; and included diverse cultural backgrounds. The services included two children's centres that provided integrated education, care and health services to children and their families; one long day care centre; two preschools; three out-of-school-hours care services; one special needs early learning centre; one family learning partnership programme in children's homes; one Family Day Care service; and one programme geared specifically for children in remote and isolated locations. We describe these sites and their regional profiles below.[1] In these descriptions, place names are replaced by names derived from the regions in which they were respectively located; pseudonyms are used for all participants and those to whom they refer throughout this book.

Home learning partnership programme in the Eyre and Western Region

The consultations conducted here were done in the context of a local family learning partnership programme conducted in children's homes, for families with children aged from birth to four years. The purpose of the programme is to support families' abilities to be involved with their children's learning, through play. Families eligible for this programme are those experiencing social isolation, mental health issues, learning difficulties, poverty, geographic isolation and challenging family circumstances. Indigenous families and new arrivals to Australia are given priority where possible.

This programme was located in a rural and remote region, which at the time of the study had a relatively middle-aged population profile, with above state average proportions of children (under 15 years) and people 45–64 years, and below state average proportions of youth (15–24 years) and young adults. The region experienced below average incomes and a predominance of farming and labouring occupations. At the time of the study, the general level of education and qualifications were below state average, with below average levels of school achievement and post-school qualifications.

18 Inquiry into the Children's Voices Project

Limestone Town kindergarten and rural care in the Limestone Coast Region

This site was a preschool and rural care service for children birth to five years in a small rural town (population 2,200 at the time of the study) geographically isolated from major centres. The preschool was integrated with its rural care service provided to the community. There was a strong emphasis on family and community partnerships, with high levels of parent and community involvement in the services provided. The preschool programme placed priority on children's literacy (including oral literacy), numeracy and wellbeing.

Limestone Town's rural regional setting comprised a relatively young population profile at the time of the study, with above state average proportions of children (under 15 years) and people aged 25–44 years. The region enjoyed above average labour force participation rates and low unemployment levels. Agriculture, forestry and fishing, and manufacturing dominated the local labour market. General level of education and qualifications were below state average, with comparatively low levels of school achievement and post-school qualifications. There were varying income levels and high proportions of owner-occupied houses, and average levels of income support recipients.

Children's centre and out-of-school-hours care in the Western Adelaide Region

This suburban site was a purpose-built children's centre for early childhood development and parenting, and part of a birth to Year 12 (post-compulsory schooling) college. Also involved in the consultations at this site were children and staff of the college's out-of-school-hours care service. Valued community membership and partnerships among educators, families and communities were emphasised in the design and delivery of the centre's programmes.

The centre's broader suburban region had a relatively middle-aged population profile at the time of the study, with above state average proportions of people aged 25–44 years and older people (65 years and over). The region experienced below average labour force participation rates, and fluctuating unemployment levels. Residents' occupations were mainly professional, semi-professional and clerical in nature. General level of education and qualifications were more or less roughly equal to state average, with slightly above average levels of school achievement and post-school qualifications. Income levels were below average and there were above average levels of income support recipients for some of the major benefits.

Family day care service in the Murray and Mallee Region

This site was a family day care provider (that is, a home-based childcare service run by a qualified early childhood educator) for children two to five years, located in an historic riverside town 100 km from the state's capital city, with a population around 2,000 people.

This small group service provided an early childhood programme in the educator's home setting, with four children under the age of five, plus three school-aged children at any given time. The service had flexible care hours catering to parents' needs, including overnight and weekend service provision.

This service's broader regional setting had a mixed population profile, with above average proportions of children (under 15 years) and people aged 45 years or more. There were below average labour force participation rates, and unemployment levels were increasing at the time of the study. Agriculture was the predominant employing industry, with significant decreases in employment since 2001. General level of education qualifications were below state average, with low levels of school achievement and post-school qualifications. Below average incomes and high levels of income support contributed to economic disadvantage in this region.

Out-of-school-hours care service in the Fleurieu Peninsula and Kangaroo Island Region

This site was an out-of-school-hours-care service for children five to twelve years in a regional location. At the time of the study, this service operated at three local primary schools and serviced the families and children from two local co-educational colleges. Drawing on Australia's national framework for out-of-school-hours care, *My time, our place* (DEEWR, 2011), educators worked with school-aged children to extend and enrich their wellbeing and learning through leisure and play experiences, complementing learning in children's home and school settings.

In this service's regional rural and coastal setting, there were above average proportions of people aged 50 and over, with below state average labour force participation rates and below state average unemployment levels at the time of the study. There were mainly managerial, associate professional, trades and labourer occupations. General level of education and qualifications were below state average, with comparatively low levels of school achievement and post-school qualifications.

Community children's centre and outreach preschool in the Southern Adelaide Region

This service was a community-based, not-for-profit children's centre and outreach preschool for children six weeks to six years in a suburban location. Staff and management worked in partnership with parents to provide quality care and education for children across developmental domains, with a strong focus on children's wellbeing. The service provided a play-based curriculum, enhanced by large natural outdoor spaces and parent involvement in the governing council.

20 Inquiry into the Children's Voices Project

At the time of the study, there was a relatively young population profile in this service's broader suburban region, with above average proportions of young adults (15–24 years) and people aged between 45–64 years. This pattern was accompanied by high proportions of families with children.

Labour force participation rates were above average and unemployment levels were low. Occupations were mainly professional, semi-professional, and clerical in nature. The general level of education and qualifications were above state average, with above average levels of school achievement and post-school qualifications. Income levels were above average, with high proportions of houses mortgaged, and below average levels of income support recipients.

Out-of-school-hours care services in the Adelaide Hills Region

At the time of the study, this community-based service was located at four primary school sites in an outer metropolitan area. The service catered to primary school-aged children in the local district needing care before and after school hours, during school holidays and on pupil-free school days.

Families and children accessed this service on a casual, part-time, regular or emergency basis. The service provided a range of recreational and leisure activities that enriched and complemented children's home and school experiences, framed by Australia's *My time, our place* out-of-school-hours care framework (DEEWR, 2011).

The outer metropolitan region in which this service was located was characterised by a relatively middle-aged population profile, with above average proportions of children under 15 and people aged 45–64 years. At the time of the study, there were high proportions of families with children and above average labour force participation rates, with low unemployment levels. Residents were highly represented in professional, semi-professional, managerial and trades occupations. The general level of education and qualifications were above the state average, with high levels of school achievement and post-school qualifications. The region experienced above average income levels and below average levels of income support recipients.

Special early learning centre in the Eastern Adelaide Region

This service was a special education preschool facility catering to children with complex health care needs. The centre was supplied support officers by a health service that catered to children, youth, parents and carers and worked directly with family members to ensure their children received health support programmes that were tailored to the child's needs.

At the time of the consultations, the metropolitan area in which this service was located featured a relatively middle-aged population, with above average proportions of youth (15–24 years) and people 45–64 years. There were below average proportions of families with children and above average labour force participation rates, with low unemployment levels. Residents were highly represented in professional, semi-professional and managerial occupations. The general level of education and qualifications were above the state average, with high levels of school achievement and post-school qualifications. Income levels were above state average, while income support recipients were below state average levels.

Children's service for remote and isolated communities in the Far North Region

This service was established in the 1970s to support families and children in meeting the challenges of living in remote and isolated areas – what is termed 'the Outback' in Australia. The service provides resources, education, childcare and support for these children and their families.

The service had its base in a seaside town that is also a rail and road junction. From this town, service staff travelled thousands of kilometres a year to provide a range of programmes and resources to families living across 650,000 square kilometres of South Australia. This provision included outback childcare, preschool education, play days, toy and book libraries, parenting resources and support through a child and family worker.

The region in which the service's base was situated had a relatively young population profile at the time of the study, with above average proportions of children and people aged between 25 and 44 years. There were above average proportions of single parents and people living alone. Labour force participation rates were below state average, with above average unemployment levels. Residents' work was predominantly in associate professional, trades, production and labouring occupations. The general level of education and qualifications were below the state average, with low levels of school achievement and post-school qualifications. There was a wide diversity of economic security, from very high to below average incomes seen across the region. There were also above average proportions of rented dwellings and income support recipients.

Children's centre in the Northern Adelaide Region

This early childhood service was a children's centre focused on catering to Indigenous Australian families and children birth to eight years, with the aim of enhancing educational outcomes for Indigenous children. Early childhood professionals, families and the local community worked together in this space, and brought together a range of education, care, health and family support services. The service included a preschool education programme and provided vocational training and parenting programmes to indigenous parents. Other programmes

22 Inquiry into the Children's Voices Project

included playgroups, mental health programmes and cooking classes to support parenting skills.

At the time of the study, the region in which this service was located was profiled by a relatively young population, with above average proportions of younger people (less than 45 years), and a particularly high percentage of school-aged children (5–14 years). There were high proportions of families with children. Labour force participation rates were mixed, with above average unemployment levels. Occupations were characterised by intermediate clerical, sales and services, and trades and trades-related work, with relatively few residents employed in higher-level occupations compared with the state average. The general level of education and qualifications were below state average, with relatively low levels of school achievement and post-school qualifications. Income levels were mixed, with high proportions of houses with mortgages and above state average levels of income support recipients.

Child–parent centre and Aboriginal school in the Yorke and Mid-North Region

This service was a child–parent centre and Aboriginal school located in a rural and remote setting. The programme was founded on values related to fairness and equity, with an educational emphasis on literacy and embedding the local Aboriginal culture and language in the curriculum, with a view to fostering children's sense of cultural pride and identity. The programme relied on a co-operative partnership with the town and district's community, in which educators, families and community members worked together to provide a safe and caring learning environment and to achieve positive outcomes.

At the time of the study, the service's regional population featured above average proportions of older people (45 years and over), with low proportions of families with children, reflecting the older age profile of the region, although there were above average proportions of children under 15 years. The region experienced higher than state average unemployment and below average participation in the labour force. General level of education and qualifications were below state average, with comparatively low levels of school achievement and post-school qualifications (which may have been a reflection of the relatively low proportions of younger people in the region). Workforce participation was below average, with unemployment and income support levels above the state average.

Procedures for gathering and analysing data

The consultations were documented through *in situ* observations at each early childhood site; collection, copying or photographing and analysis of artefacts created by children during the consultations; analysis of key documents relevant to and developed from the consultations; interviews with government

Inquiry into the Children's Voices Project 23

personnel; and participant observation. These methods are described below, followed by a description of how the four case studies were documented, and an account of the ways and means that trustworthiness of this case study inquiry was assured.

Observations

The educators facilitating the consultations in their own sites documented these consultations through means they chose to best suit their own contexts. Running records and anecdotal records were developed at the sites, which became ongoing foci for staff reflection as they continued to plan and refine their particular consultation process. Video- and audio-recordings were also used; and staff at one site produced two DVDs from their recordings. Photographs of children's engagement and creations were also taken across the sites.

Educators documented and synthesised their observations in their final reports that they submitted to DECS after the consultations ended. All reports provided a description of the site's context and how the consultations were approached. Photographs and photocopies of children's engagement and creations were included, along with direct extracts of what children said during their engagement and the educators' own reflections on the process.

Artefacts

The artefacts included in this study's data were photographs of children's engagement in the consultations; originals, photocopies or photographs of children's works (including drawings, paintings and photos children themselves took); and the public exhibition of children's original works at a special gallery presentation that lasted two weeks. This material was analysed in terms of identifying and categorising children's themes of interest and concern.

Document analysis

The following key documents were collected and analysed, using emergent thematic analysis:

- DECS Induction package, which was provided to educators to support and guide their implementation of the consultations with children at their respective sites.
- Educators' final reports of their consultations with children in their respective services, which they provided to DECS. These reports contained overviews of the consultations, the processes involved, and the views children conveyed, including children's own words and copies of their expressive, multi-modal creations such as photographs, drawings, paintings, dioramas, captions and personal commentaries, and recordings of dance, movement and song.

24 Inquiry into the Children's Voices Project

- DECS final report of the consultations with children, which was published on the DECS website, distributed among all participants, made available to those who attended the gallery exhibition of the consultations, and provided to DPC for their deliberations on strategic priorities.
- Community Engagement Board Report that incorporated findings from community consultations, including those with young children.

Interviews with government personnel

Interviews were conducted with DECS and DPC personnel involved in the consultations. These interviews were audio-recorded and transcribed. The following questions were asked:

- How did this initiative come about?
- Why was there a wish to engage with young children?
- Who were the stakeholders in these consultations?
- How did DECS and DPC work together? How did this collaboration take shape?
- How did you see your role in this process?
- How did you go about planning these consultations? What were key considerations in this planning?
- How did you organise for the consultations to be done?
- What support was required and what support was provided for these consultations to occur?
- (For DECS) How did the sites' educators report the outcomes of their children's consultations to you?
- (For DECS) How did you go about making sense of this information?
- (For DECS) How did you report this information and communicate it to DPC?
- Do you consider that the consultations were successful or not? In what ways? What contributed to this success?
- What would you change if you were to do this again?
- (For DPC) How was the information from DECS organised and packaged for you?
- (For DPC) What were the key points of interest that you found in the DECS report?
- (For DPC) Did this information meet your needs and the broader needs of the DPC?
- Are there any other comments you'd like to make?

Participant observation

Given Harris' involvement as adviser and researcher in the consultations, she adopted the role of participant observer to document the planning and development of consultation strategies in which she was involved, as well as the induction workshop for educators that she led to assist educators in developing and implementing their consultation strategies. Participant observation data were recorded as anecdotal records and reflections kept in the researcher's journal.

Embedded case studies

At the outset of the consultations, four sites were involved in more in-depth case study inquiry into the consultations. These sites were: Limestone Kindergarten and Rural Care in the Limestone Coast Region; the Home Learning Partnership Programme in the Eyre and Western Region; the Out-of-School Hours Care service in the Fleurieu and Kangaroo Island Region; and the Children's Centre and Out-of-School Hours Care service in the Western Adelaide region. These sites were chosen by virtue of their informed consent and because together they represented a range of service types; a range of localities (one suburban, one rural, one regional and one remote); and demographics as previously described.

The purpose of the case studies was two-fold: (i) to understand what it means to be early childhood educators fully engaged with children as valued active citizens; and (ii) to account for the complexities of this participation as they unfolded over time in a context where consulting with children as citizens to inform policy directions had not been the norm.

Accordingly, the case studies provided a means for probing more deeply the efficacy of the consultations from a Freirean perspective of enacting children's citizenship and valuing their voice in dialogic encounters in and about their world. In keeping with such a perspective, there were five conceptual categories explored in each case study site, which are described below.

Framing the consultations

How educators framed the consultations was of interest in these case studies. Examining this framing revealed educators' initial preconceptions, struggles and deliberations that they brought to the planning stage of the consultations; how they framed the purpose of the consultations for engagement with children; the problems they posed as they thought about how to approach the consultations; how educators posed the problem at hand in terms of children contributing their views about what they liked and did not like in their local communities and what they wished for in their lives; and how educators found themselves confronting their own roles and the perceived limitations of their children and themselves.

Nature of the dialogic encounter in the consultations

Exploring the nature of the encounter between educator and child in the consultations involved looking at how and to what extent children and educators adopted the roles of co-constructors of meaning. Such consideration extended to examining educators' release of control to children while supporting their participation in dialogue in and about their local worlds; and raising children's awareness of their own communities through multi-modal and play-based exploration, interrogation and expression of their viewpoints.

Structures and modes that sustained dialogue and depth of meaning

Structures and modes that enabled or constrained the consultations as dialogic encounters in and about children's worlds were carefully examined. Such consideration included educators' use and transformation of time frames, interaction patterns and participant structures, which re-framed day-to-day interactions as co-construction between children and educators, parents and other adults who facilitated and scaffolded the consultations. Children's multiple modes of exploration, interrogation and expression also were examined, as was the further development of children's and educators' expertise in these modes to give voice to children's thoughts and actions.

Documenting children's voices and words

How educators documented children's voices and words was examined. As importantly, how authenticity of this documentation was assured was also examined, in terms of validly and reliably documenting what the young children actually said and expressed and their intended meaning. Key emergent themes related to the challenges and imperatives educators experienced in striving to understand and maintain the integrity of children's voices in their documentation, and the struggle many educators found in interpreting children's intended meaning not *for* but *with* the child. The messages that children conveyed and which were captured in this documentation were also examined and thematised.

Empowerment and conscientisation

This category of understanding related to child and educator alike. For children, this category related to children's enthusiastic will and depth of engagement that came from knowing their voices were being heard, understood and acted upon. For educators, this category related to educators' professional identities and their sense of self not only as educators but as human beings in dialogic encounters with young children as co-learners – and what releasing control to the children meant for educators' own sense of empowerment.

Documenting the case studies

The observations for the case studies were the same as those previously described for the overall consultation above. However, the analysis of the observational data more deeply probed the data from the standpoint of examining the effectiveness of the consultations in terms of the five conceptual categories explained above.

In-depth, semi-structured interviews provided the means for exploring educators' perspectives of the consultations that they conducted with the young children in their early childhood sites. The interviews were audio-recorded and transcribed. Interview questions explored how educators implemented and documented the consultations; what they found worked well and what could be improved; what challenges arose; and how children engaged. Specifically the following questions were asked:

- Tell me, how did you find this strategy work with children?
- What if anything seemed to work well?
- What if anything was difficult or challenging in using this approach?
- What if anything might you change to improve this strategy?
- In your opinion did the children engage well and provide some insightful responses?
- Looking at your documentation of the consultations, can you explain a little of the process of the documentation and your thought processes as you put this together?
- What if any were some of the challenges you found as you put this documentation together?
- What interpretations of children's words and ideas did you find yourself making and what did you base these interpretations on?
- What interpretations of children's products did you find yourself making and what did you base these interpretations on?
- Is there anything that you'd do differently in the documentation next time?
- Are there any other comments that you'd like to make?

Interview data were thematised using emergent interpretive techniques (Glesne, 2006). The broad themes that emerged related to the impact of the consultations on educators' own practices; children's engagement with the consultations; challenges that arose; things that worked well; and things that could be improved or done differently. These themes were related to the five conceptual categories previously described. This analysis was triangulated with observations, document analyses and artefact collections within each case study.

As with the Children's Voices Project in its entirety, children's words and other meaning-making creations (e.g. paintings, drawings, photographs) were collected and copied or photographed for these case studies. This material was analysed in terms of the thoughts and actions these artefacts gave voice to, and the broader thematic concerns for children that they represented.

Educators at each case study site, in collaboration with their colleagues and children, developed an in-depth report of the consultations, as previously described. These reports contained comprehensive written accounts of the site's approach to and implementation of the consultations; key messages from children in their own words and further interpreted by the site's educators; and illustrative material including children's work samples and scribed text, photographs and video-recordings of their engagement. These reports were provided to DECS, and for the purposes of the case studies, collected and analysed using emergent interpretive techniques (Glesne, 2006), with themes mapped onto the nested case studies' five conceptual categories.

Ensuring trustworthiness

As the consultations occurred simultaneously across geographically widespread sites, it was not possible to directly observe the consultations as they occurred. It was important, therefore, to ensure trustworthy documentation through multiple and rigorous means, as described above. Triangulation across these data collection methods contributed to the study's trustworthiness, as did triangulation across different participants and sites in the study and the use of digital recordings (audio, video and still photography).

Given this book's first author's (Harris) role as adviser to the consultations process and a participant observer in the planning and induction phases of the consultations, a number of additional trustworthiness measures were taken. The researcher maintained a reflective journal; undertook member-checking with participants in a focal group discussion at the end of the consultations; debriefed with colleagues throughout the research process; and employed a research assistant removed from the consultations to conduct the interviews, analyse data and crosscheck data analysis with the researcher.

It is to the findings of this case study inquiry into the Children's Voices Project that we now turn – beginning with the planning and professional development phases.

Note

1. This regional profile information was derived at the time of the study from the South Australian website at http://www.workforceinfoservice.sa.gov.au/regionalprofiles (retrieved 18 January 2012).

Chapter 3

Planning to engage with children as active citizens

A humanising education is the path through which men and women can become conscious about their presence in the world.

(Freire and Frei Betto, 1985, p. 14)

Awakening conscious awareness of children's presence as valued active citizens in the world systematically began in the Children's Voices Project with the acknowledgment by policymakers, educators and children alike that children are citizens in the here and now, with agency and the capacity to contribute to decision-making processes. The consultations with children were framed as dialogic encounter and focused on the central question: 'What is important to children in their communities and what do children wish for in their lives?'

Moving beyond tokenism in children's participation

In planning the consultations as dialogic encounter with children, there was a conscious and explicit desire to move beyond tokenistic gestures and lip-service actions. No matter how well intentioned, there is an inherent danger when involving children in community matters traditionally seen as the domain of adults – that the value of children's participation will be diminished to a self-contained activity for educational purposes, rather than recognising the value children's democratic participation provides the whole community.

As Brett (2007) found in the UK schools context, while students had opportunities to exercise their citizenship, these experiences generally were confined to the school context and were more about taking part in an experience rather than to effect change by engaging in decision-making processes. Brett also found that such involvement usually was confined to certain groups of students and not to all students (despite all students being invited to participate); and that students' participation did not systematically connect beyond their school with broader community contexts. Indeed, Hart's ladder of participation (1992) describes most attempts to engage children as essentially forms of 'non-participation' and challenges an improvement in genuine practices to move beyond 'tokenism' in children's participation to true citizenship.

30 Planning to engage with children as active citizens

Involving young children in matters of public planning can be met with scepticism about the abilities and value children bring to public policy decision-making, given children's perceived limited knowledge of the intricacies of adult decision-making processes. The challenge, then, for the Children's Voices Project, was to move beyond a tokenistic involvement of children to a meaningful and valued partnership.

In order to integrate children's valued participation in the community, the process needed to be seen to be as important as the outcome. Foregrounding process was important to children's effective engagement, in turn assisting adults in seeing the importance of children as valued citizens in the here and now, rather than only citizens of the future. Emphasising process is also a matter of respectful engagement with children, characterised by transparency and accountability that help develop and retain children's faith in democratic processes, making it more likely for children to value their participation as adults (Invernizzi and Williams, 2008).

It was clear from the outset of the Children's Voices Project that, for children's participation to be meaningful in shaping the strategic plan for the state of South Australia, a cultural shift would need to happen. The 2011 review of children's participation policy by the Council of Europe recognises that the biggest hindrance in meaningful consultation with children lies in the attitudes of adults (Council of Europe, 2011). Such a cultural shift would need to reframe societal perceptions of children as future leaders with limited experience with their community surroundings beyond the family or educational environment, to a recognition of children as competent and capable individuals. While achieving a cultural shift across the whole of society would not be possible in the Children's Voices Project's time frame, the Project was seen to be an important beginning to working towards higher quality practices that would foster a sustained commitment in South Australia to children's valued, active citizenship.

At first glance, such a cultural shift would need to occur primarily with those sectors of society responsible for community planning but who are not directly involved with children's services, programmes or facilities. Perceptions that children could not contribute meaningfully would need to be reframed. An example often given by those attempting meaningful consultation with children arises in the context of fast food outlets. It can be easy for an adult to dismiss children's assertions that more fast food outlets are needed in the community due to health and nutritional concerns. However, when time is taken to explore and understand why children are identifying fast food restaurants, what is generally found is that children's interest does not lay so much with the food itself. Instead, children's concerns rest with social interactions with family and other children enjoyed in such places, as well as having access to the children's games, play equipment and activities provided at these venues (Hobsons Bay Council, 2009).

A cultural shift also would need to foster recognition that children's lives are impacted not only by their particular family, education and health circumstances – but also broader social, economic and environmental factors that impact us all. For example, urban planning impacts on children's physical activity and health. Likewise, the economy and job security impact on family stability and stress factors in the home environment, which in turn affect children's wellbeing. Social, economic and environmental benefits of investing in children from a young age are well documented. This research includes the work of Nobel Laureate and economist Professor James Heckman; and physician and scientist, the late Dr James Fraser Mustard, among other distinguished academics and researchers who recognise benefits ranging from increased productivity, economic growth and social stability (Heckman and Masterov, 2007; Mustard, 2007).

What was less evident at the outset of the Children's Voices Project was that cultural change needed to apply equally to those already working closely with children, such as educators, parents and policy makers in child centered fields. The extraordinary practices within education and care settings between children and adult educators would need to traverse the boundaries of educational settings and be more broadly integrated with the community. Those most experienced in working with children would need to move beyond seeing themselves as experts on children, to seeing themselves also as advocates for and partners with children. To merely advocate for children on their behalf without meaningfully eliciting their views to inform action based on these views could diminish children's perceived competence and devalue the importance of reconceptualising children across society as competent citizens.

With these challenges in mind, a number of key considerations were identified in the planning of South Australia's Children's Voices Project. These considerations included developing a shared and explicit appreciation of the importance of children's voice, which entailed reframing others' thinking as doing *with* rather than *for* children. There was strong consensus that children's authentic voices would be engaged – that these consultations would be consequential and beneficial in involving children in significant decision-making processes, based on the recognition that children are citizens now and deserve the right to be heard.

A number of pragmatic questions were also discussed:

- Who is to be involved?
- How do we want people to be involved?
- How will we support their involvement?
- How will we foster meaningful relationships among those involved?
- How many children can/should we involve?
- Will we engage with educators and if so, in what ways and with whom?
- What expertise is available on which we can draw?
- What support is provided to implement the consultations (e.g., time, equipment, expertise, materials, other), and who will provide this support and how?
- How will we implement and document the consultations?

Identifying purpose of the Children's Voices Project

It was important to clearly identify and articulate the purpose of the Children's Voices Project in terms of informing action, so as to ensure authenticity of the encounter. Consequently, the threefold purpose of the consultations with children was identified as follows:

- To ensure our youngest citizens were provided with a valued voice in informing the review of South Australia's Strategic Plan and the development of a 'Child Friendly South Australia', aligned with the *UNICEF Child Friendly Cities Framework*.
- To research, document and develop tools of best practice to support future endeavours to meaningfully include children in public planning.
- To publicly showcase the value and possibilities of linking children's learning about civics and citizenship to real-life opportunities to participate in decision-making within children's communities.

Engaging non-traditional partners

A significant challenge in the planning phase of the Children's Voices' Project concerned the involvement of individuals and organisations not traditionally engaging with children directly, but whose policies or decisions impact on children's lives.

To assist in changing attitudes and cultural perspectives, individuals in organisations or sectors who value and understand the benefits of children's participation were sought out. Strong relationships with these people were developed to help influence cultural change in and across their respective organisations and sectors. The Children's Voices project brought together a team of advocates to take carriage of planning the consultations and establishing links and partnerships with their respective networks. The central planning team were the de Lissa Chair in Early Childhood Research (and first named author of this book); the Director of Strategic Initiatives within DECS; the Senior Policy Adviser in this team (and second author of this book); the Manager of Community Engagement and Consultations for the State Strategic Plan; and a DECS Early Childhood Adviser from the Early Years Learning team.

In inviting appropriate individuals and organisations to take ownership and contribute to the professional development associated with the Children's Voices Project, links between research, policy and practice outlined in Figure 3.1 were considered.

The planning team recognised that the success of the consultations would also rely in no small measure on the enthusiasm, expertise and goodwill of all participating staff and partners, particularly the educators working directly with children. Supporting each service in their implementation and documentation of the consultations emerged as a key priority. The Early Childhood Adviser

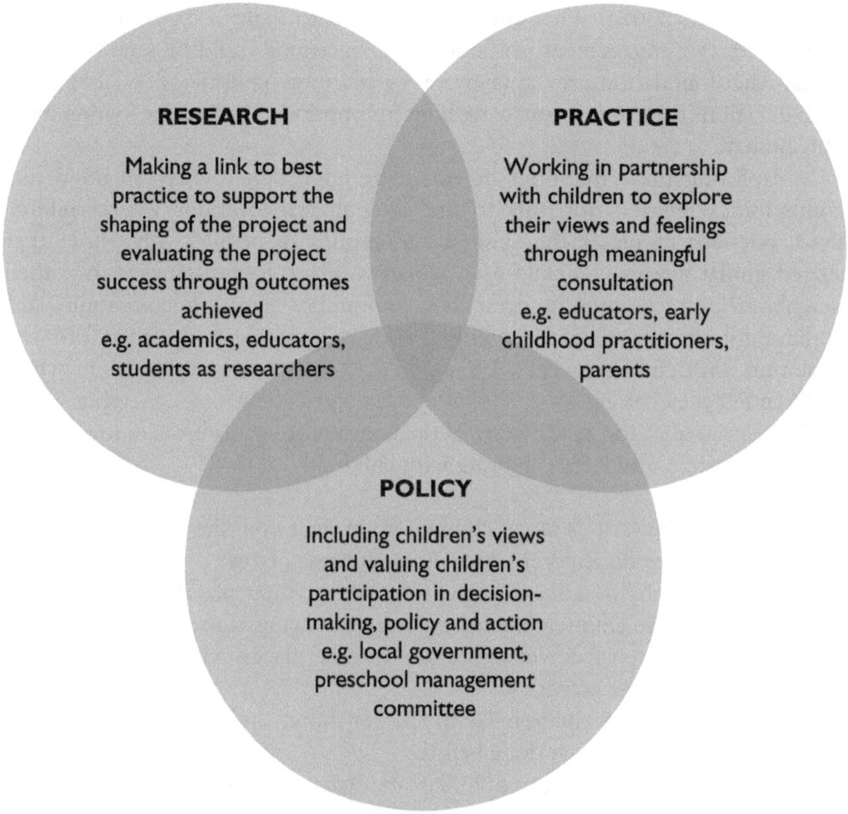

RESEARCH

Making a link to best practice to support the shaping of the project and evaluating the project success through outcomes achieved
e.g. academics, educators, students as researchers

PRACTICE

Working in partnership with children to explore their views and feelings through meaningful consultation
e.g. educators, early childhood practitioners, parents

POLICY

Including children's views and valuing children's participation in decision-making, policy and action
e.g. local government, preschool management committee

Figure 3.1 Connecting research, policy and practice

from the Early Years Learning team was available for educators working with children as required. Material support also was provided through small grants afforded by DPC for centres to purchase materials and equipment needed in the consultations.

Formulating the core theme of the consultations

With the values, pragmatic considerations and purpose of the consultations in mind, and after considerable deliberations among the planning group, the focal question for these statewide consultations became, 'What is important to children in their communities and what do children wish for in their lives?' This question resonates with such questions that lie at the heart of citizenship education from a Freirean perspective – questions like, 'What sort of society do we live in?', 'What kind of society and world do we want to live in in the future?' and 'What can

34 Planning to engage with children as active citizens

I and others do to change things and make a difference to the world that we live in?' (Brett, 2007). What children might do to make a difference was not considered, but engagement in the first two questions could be seen over time to lay the foundations for this more far-reaching consideration. Exploring such questions over time resonate with Freire's notion (1983) of becoming more fully human.

In exploring these questions, it would be important to keep in mind that communities referred not only to the geographical locations where children lived, but also to places they visited and groups of people with whom they shared similar interests. A child may be part of many communities such as their neighbourhood community, preschool community, sporting community, the community where their grandparents live. A key starting point, therefore, was exploring with children what a community is and the communities in which children felt they belong.

The central question at the heart of the consultations was broken down into a range of possible topics for exploring with children:

- Where are the various places children go in their everyday lives?
- What activities do children enjoy doing at these places?
- Who do the children like to spend time with at these places?
- What things do children like seeing or experiencing at these places?
- How do children feel when they are at these places, with these people, or undertaking these activities?
- What places would children like to visit, or things they would like to see and do that they have never done before?
- What places do children not like and what things do they not enjoy, and why?

Developing conversations with children around these kinds of questions were valued by the planning team for not only informing the vision for a child-friendly state, but also for validating children's right to have a voice about matters that directly affect their lives now and in the future as affirmed in the UN Convention on the Rights of the Child (United Nations, 1989) – matters at the heart of legitimating children's citizenship and democratic participation.

The UN Convention on the Rights of the Child in regard to children's voice and participation continued to emerge during this planning phase:

> All people, however young, are entitled to be participants in their own lives, to influence what happens to them, to be involved in creating their own environments, to exercise choices and to have their views respected and valued.
>
> (Lansdown, 2005, p. 40, cited in DECS, 2010, p. 8)

A final consideration for the planning team was the idea of exploring places where children did not like to go and things they did not like doing. If, for example, children identified that they did not like going to restaurants with their families, it would be useful to understand why. Could it be, for example, that there are no children's activities at these locations? Care would need be taken to ensure children would be comfortable with discussing things they did not like and ensuring the themes explored were not likely to cause any distress. South Australian guidelines relating to child safety would need to be referred to if any such issues arose.

Consultation strategies

How the consultation theme would be operationalised within meaningful consultations with young children – children as young as three years of age – emerged as a significant challenge in this planning phase. As civics and citizenship are key learning areas of most modern day curricula and learning frameworks, the planning team decided to programme the consultations in direct relation to *Belonging, being and becoming: the early years learning framework for Australia* (DEEWR, 2009).

Subsequent conversations focused on how to engage children's voices through multi-modal means that go beyond verbal interactions alone and are challenging and enjoyable for children – and which take children's minds seriously. To these ends, recourse was made to the literature and to participants' own tacit understandings about young children's capacities for expressing their ideas.

Developing consultation strategies drew on current understandings about the multiple modes of language and literacy through which young children express themselves through many and varied ways – such as evoked in Malaguzzi's 'hundred languages of children' (Edwards *et al.*, 2012) and including talking, drawing, painting, computer technology, photography, construction, music, dance, drama, collage, sculptures, movement, storytelling, pretend play and socio-dramatic play (Harris, 2009; Makin *et al.*, 2007). In consequence, six consultation strategies were planned, with each participating children's service to be given one strategy to further develop and implement.

The first strategy was engaging children through movement and role play. This was to engage children in the development of short performances which demonstrate through movement, story telling and role play children's views about the consultation theme. This would include children's services educators working with performing artists.

As a second strategy, children were to engage through digital photography and information technology, which would provide an opportunity for children to express views about the consultation theme, through children's use of digital cameras with adults and their descriptions of what the photos represented to the child. This strategy was developed to be particularly conducive to children's participation in remote and rural locations and to promote the role of parents/ grandparents and guardians in encouraging children to have an active voice in their communities.

The third strategy was engaging children through art, by encouraging children to express their views through a visual artistic medium. Various options were identified as possibilities for educators to consider, including the painting of a mural, a sculpture, woodcarving or other means (dependent on the interests of the children). Engagement of local artists to assist with this process was also identified as a possibility.

A fourth strategy was children's engagement through music, dance and song. This strategy was to encourage children to express views through song and/or dance with the possibility of musical instruments also being incorporated to develop a musical or dance performance.

Engagement through themed drawing and painting became the fifth strategy, focusing on children expressing their views through diagrams, pictures, drawings and paintings about a specific theme. Adults or children themselves were to be encouraged to include a short written description on the drawing or painting of what the picture represents, capturing the children's explanation of their drawing in their own words.

The final strategy was to focus on engagement of children through story telling. A number of opportunities were identified for consideration of participants, including children undertaking a walking tour or treasure hunt in the community while developing a narrative about their experience, or involving adults working with children, such as a grandparent and child each telling a part of a story that reflects the child's views.

These strategies were not defined in detail, to provide space for educators to exercise their well-informed professional judgments about what would work with their particular children in their sites, drawing on available resources to support this engagement.

The planning team was emphatic that these strategies should be inclusive of all children, including children with additional needs. It therefore was important that educators consider adapting strategies to best suit their participating children. The involvement of families and educators who know children well was seen as the best approach to ensuring the most effective strategies for specific children. In the case of children unable to communicate, the planning team thought it useful to engage with more than one adult who knows the child well to corroborate understanding of the child's intended meaning.

Providing professional development

The next phase of planning involved professional development for all partners participating in the project. Professional development in any setting was seen to be a valuable means of exchanging information and ideas, aligning the focus of all contributors to similar outcomes and supporting individuals to grow their knowledge and skills. Even those well versed in engaging with young children are able to benefit from self-reflection by deepening their understanding of their own knowledge and practices, and challenging themselves to reflect more deeply on their practices with young children.

Planning to engage with children as active citizens   37

This professional development was planned to occur before, during and after the consultations with children. It provided an opportunity for all involved in the Children's Voices Project to come together across disciplines and fields of expertise and arrive at some common understandings and ownership of the project's processes and outcomes.

This professional development was underpinned by the recognition that all attendees had individual skills and knowledge to contribute to the learning process, with facilitators and participants alike continuing to share and grow through a cycle of continuous learning. The skills and expertise gained through the project, then, were able to be shared further within the community to facilitate further projects and processes involving children's voices and active participation.

Figure 3.2 highlights the continuous cycle of learning that framed this professional development. Each of these stages identified in this figure is described in further detail below.

Developing an induction package

In order to support an engaging and successful induction workshop, an induction package was developed to guide the content of the workshop and to provide a resource for reference and guidance following the workshop. As both the

Figure 3.2 The continuous cycle of professional development

38 Planning to engage with children as active citizens

induction resources and induction workshop explored the same content, each is described briefly before considering some of the content of both the resources and workshop in greater detail.

The approach taken in planning the workshop was consultative and inclusive of the rich diversity of views and expertise of those attending. Consequently, the induction package was designed not to be overly prescriptive. Instead, the induction materials were provided as a guide to stimulate further conversation and ensure shared understanding of the Children's Voices Project's purpose, processes and desired outcomes, as well as non-negotiable matters such as informed consent, voluntary participation and privacy.

The induction resource booklet provided a rationale for the inclusion of young children in the statewide consultations, in terms of valuing children's voices and active participation. Explicit links were made to the United Nation's Convention on the Rights of the Child in terms of ensuring shared understanding of the mandate for undertaking consultations with children. Guidance was given regarding the importance of identifying the purpose of the consultations, so as to be clear as to why the consultation with children was to be taking place, the context in which the opportunity had arisen, and the value it would contribute to individuals, organisations and communities as a whole.

The induction resources contextualised the consultations in terms of the three themes of being, belonging and becoming in Australia's *Early years learning framework* (DEEWR, 2009) referred to in Chapter 1 – specifically in relation to children's participation in their local communities. This link was further distilled in the key focal question: 'What is important to children in their communities and what do they wish for in their lives?' The booklet unpacked this question with a number of contributing questions considered earlier in this chapter. Strategies for implementing the consultations were described, with scope for educators using these strategies to further develop them in ways they saw fit in their own contexts (again described earlier in this chapter). The description of these strategies and the overall spirit in which these consultations were to be conducted was further supported in the booklet's inclusion of case studies of consultations with other *albeit* older children.

The next section of the resource booklet provided 'useful tips' that highlighted key principles for consulting with children. These tips focused on the importance of the process as much as the product; explaining to children how and why they are being involved; using community photos taken from children's eye levels; accurately recording what children say and do, with the support of digital recording and photographs where possible; asking lead questions and providing prompts to encourage children's elaboration on their ideas; using projection techniques such as 'What do you think . . .?' and 'How do you feel . . .?'; acknowledging the power difference between adult and child and indeed, the child and the child's educator; accounting for and being mindful of the dynamic among children in group situations; and providing feedback to children about what will happen after the consultations have finished. Information sheets and consent forms for children's parents were appended, as were lists of print-based and online resources.

The induction workshop

The induction workshop saw participants and partners come together and meet face-to-face to gain a deeper understanding of the opportunities and constraints each was faced with. The workshop provided a valuable forum at which participants aligned outcomes, strategies and resources and took ownership in co-operatively shaping the project. Of course, there was also opportunity to address any issues or concerns that individuals raised. The in-person nature of the induction workshop also facilitated relationships among those attending and created a strong network of support between those individuals and organisations.

In determining who to invite, the role each individual would play was considered. Essential roles included a project manager, project sponsors, local champions, mentors, a research leader, a public policy leader and consultation facilitators.

The project manager (Manatakis) co-ordinated the planning and linking the various aspects of the project, including fostering meaningful relationships between the partners involved. This role was essential to ensure overall cohesion of the project while recognising the collective expertise of all partners and participants.

Project sponsors and public policy leaders were identified as those individuals from organisations supporting the project in terms of staff time, resources, promotion and other support. These included senior management from DECS and DPC that would be able to influence the uptake of children's messages in future decision making. It was important these individuals be part of the process right from the induction phase to ensure they gained a deeper understanding of the value of the undertaking, and the process and outcomes achievable. So doing ensured a greater likelihood of the views of children being followed through into action and also increased the likelihood of the sponsors embedding children's participation practices within their organisations rather than the undertaking simply being seen as a one-off project.

Having local champions participate in the workshop also was seen to be beneficial, as their influence and respect in the wider community could further promote children as valued citizens. Local champions who attended the workshop were Early Childhood Consultants from DECS, working with early childhood education and care services in local communities. Other possibilities would have been also valid, such as mayors, journalists, local business owners or community leaders.

As mentor, the DECS Early Childhood Adviser from the Early Years Learning team provided expertise and support in linking the consultation strategies with the Early Years Learning Framework and so their contribution to the workshop was critical. The cycle of continuous learning outlined in Figure 3.2 identifies

40 Planning to engage with children as active citizens

that those who contributed to the Children's Voices Project could themselves become mentors for such endeavours in the future.

As the de Lissa Chair in Early Childhood Research, Harris was also an essential participant of the workshop. The linking of research to the project throughout all stages ensured that best practice was able to be documented, analysed, reported and shared. As lead researcher, the de Lissa Chair was also well placed to conduct the case study inquiry into the Children's Voices Project, so as to reflect on the value and efficacy of such engagement for all involved.

The Children's Voices Project was a partnership with early childhood services – in most cases, educators working in those services. However, in some instances – particularly in remote and isolated locations – parents were best placed to facilitate consultations with their children in the family home. In these situations, a lead co-ordinator represented parents at the workshop, and then worked closely with a range of families in a particular community to provide support throughout the journey. The value of educators or parents facilitating the consultations was underscored by their established relationships with the children who engaged in the consultations.

A final consideration for the partners coming together at the induction workshop was the choice of an appropriate facilitator. The de Lissa Chair undertook this role, given her knowledge of and advocacy for children's participation and citizenship. We recognise, however, that an effective facilitator is one who is highly skilled in drawing on the expertise of those in the room and gathered around the collective table. The key is to facilitate such a workshop in an inclusive manner, ensuring maximum engagement and sharing among participants.

It was recognised that participants at the workshop would each have a unique and preferred learning style with some people engaging better through face-to-face dialogue and others through reading and self-reflection. Written versions of the workshop's content were included, and key ideas, issues and concerns raised in discussion were documented and referred to appropriate people for advice. Activities and further information explored within the workshop were also collated and documented and provided to participants and partners following the workshop.

An interactive approach was taken to the workshop, with all participants invited to engage and share their views and co-operatively shape the strategies and approaches taken. Content was explored in a flexible and adaptable way to enable further innovation of ideas, with time allocated to discuss alternative views and address concerns.

The induction workshop unpacked each of the consultation strategies identified in the induction resource booklet, as well as explored principles that guided how these strategies might be further developed and implemented by educators for the children with whom they worked.

Ethical considerations were clarified in terms of children's voluntary participation and informed consent and assurance of the privacy and confidentiality of all involved. Of equal importance was the assurance that the experiences in which children would be engaged would be worthwhile and appropriate. Appropriateness was explored in terms of age appropriateness, cultural appropriateness and individual appropriateness.

The workshop also explored the importance of respecting the child, understanding that handing the floor to the child does not diminish adult responsibilities to the child (Woodhead and Faulkner, 2000). This respect went hand-in-hand with ensuring the consultations were conducted in the context of safe and secure relationships with children in which adults showed genuine interest in children's points of view.

Developing intersubjectivity (Rogoff, 1990) as shared understandings between children and educators during their interactions with one another was also highlighted. This understanding extended to ensuring children understood how and why they were being invited to take part in these consultations. Clarification and negotiation of what was or would be happening during the consultations were ongoing processes. In addition, the workshop emphasised the importance of feedback to children after the consultations were finished, in terms of explaining to children what would happen after their participation in the consultations, how their views have been important, and sharing what other children expressed. This feedback and follow-up was valued in terms of recognising, acknowledging and validating children's contributions, thereby enhancing their sense of self-worth, place and community.

In handing the agenda to the children for the consultations, projection techniques were explored in the workshop, which included conversation starters such as:

- 'Tell me, what do you think about . . .?'
- 'How do you feel when . . .?'
- 'What do you like about . . .?'
- 'What makes you think that?'
- 'What makes you feel that way?'

Scaffolding children to express their ideas as fully as possible was emphasised, following from the work of Wood *et al.* (1976), Vygotsky (1978) and Painter (1991) – thereby balancing children's agency with their dependency, as discussed in Chapter 1. Strategies for clarifying, extending, re-formulating and prompting children to elaborate upon their ideas, were all explored, in the context of continuing to check for shared understanding as the conversations unfolded.

Being mindful of power difference between adults and children was also considered to be important in these consultations – are the children expressing what they think or what they think adults want to hear? There can be a fine line between scaffolding and directing children's expression of ideas, and for the purpose of these consultations, it was critical that children's authentic voices were heard. The lines of conversations that were embedded in the consultation strategies needed to appropriately support the child in expressing ideas they might not be able to do on their own without putting words in their mouth – that is, create a zone of proximal development (Vygotsky, 1978) through scaffolding (Wood *et al.*, 1976) that begins with where the child is at and draws out his/her ideas. Whose interpretation of what a child says counts and how do we know that this is a fair and accurate representation of what a child intended were key considerations, addressed by ongoing processes of checking with children about what they mean.

The workshop also explored ways to enhance accurate representation and trustworthy interpretation of what children express – such as taking photos supported by drawings and talking about these images, then playing back to children what is thought they have expressed as a member-checking procedure to validate interpretations that are made. Active listening (Stephenson, 2010) was emphasised in terms of tuning into what children say and *how* they say it – their intonation, facial expressions, gestures, gaze and body language.

Germane to these deliberations is the notion of 'visible listening' (Rinaldi, 2006, p. 35), that is, 'listening which includes documentation and interpretation' (Rinaldi, 2006, p. 35). It would not be enough that these consultations engage children's voices – it would be a matter of how these voices were accurately documented, authentically interpreted and meaningfully acted upon that would be critical to the success of the consultations and genuinely respecting and enacting children's rights.

Documenting the learning journey

This professional development was itself a dialogic encounter, with the coming together of action and reflection in what Freire (1983) called praxis. Part of reflection for educators was documenting the journey, considering what they knew already and what they learned along the way. The induction workshop highlighted the importance of the learning journey by allocating time at pivotal stages throughout the day for self-reflection and documenting of individual thoughts. Such self-reflection was considered not only beneficial to those considering themselves as novices with regards to children's participation as active citizens and learners, but equally beneficial to those with extensive expertise in the area.

The induction booklet and workshop provided a series of key self-reflection questions to stimulate personal thought prior to sharing personal reflections with the broader group:

- How might we explore the consultation theme in a meaningful way with children?
- How might we document children's voices respectfully?
- Where might we begin?
- How can we make children's thinking visible to others?

- How confident do we feel about our capacity to consult with children?
- What might be the challenges to eliciting children's authentic ideas and thoughts?
- What resources/support might we need?
- How can we best utilise the financial resources?
- What documentation will we need to collect and how?

A significant aspect of self-reflection would also become evident in the documentation of the implementation strategies with children. Educators were encouraged to record the consultations through audio, video and/or photographic means and to cross-check their interpretations with the child by using reflective language – for example, 'I see you have taken lots of outdoor photos. Why's that?' It was considered very important for educators not to assume they understand what children say or create as part of these consultations. Children often talk as they work and play, even if just to themselves, and express themselves non-verbally. Educators were encouraged to tune in to all aspects of children's engagement where possible and practicable, and to note these observations for later reference to enrich records of what children conveyed and to assist with self-reflection in terms of professional development.

Educators were given scope to plan and detail how they would document the consultations within the guidelines provided. Consequently, each site took a different approach to both the consultations and their documentation while keeping in mind that the documentation benefited both the outcome and learning journey.

Guidance on ethical and legal matters

To ensure the values of a truly democratic process were reflected, throughout the induction process it was stressed that it would be essential for children's participation to be voluntary and for parent/guardian consent to be obtained for access to photos, audio or visual footage, children's artistic works and children's views.

A draft letter for parents was provided to participants, identifying the purpose of the consultations and benefits to children's learning outcomes and citizenship. The consultation theme and strategy were also outlined for parents so that they understood the activities involved and the types of issues children would be exploring. To whom this information would be given and how was clearly articulated, as was how the information would be used for public policy and planning purposes. The letter provided an assurance that children's educators would be involved and that the consultations would be incorporated within Australia's early years curriculum learning framework, without disruption to children's learning. A consent form was enclosed, providing an understanding to parents that they may limit consent to certain aspects such as allowing their child to provide their views but for photographs of their child to not be taken for example.

44 Planning to engage with children as active citizens

The consent form clarified the extent of the permission being provided – that the information from children, as well as their artistic works, photos and artefacts would be provided to DECS and DPC for the purposes of informing the review of South Australia's Strategic Plan. It was made clear that these items would also be used for promotional or educational purposes, as it would be important to strive for continual improvement in consulting with young children. Finally as mentioned in the letter to parents, the consent form provided an opportunity for parents to limit consent to certain aspects to enable adequate flexibility for children's views to be captured without concerns of privacy excluding their consideration. The draft consent forms were made available in English with staff having access to translated versions in twenty-five languages for parents or guardians of different linguistic backgrounds as part of standard practice of DECS. Despite having parent or guardian consent it was recommended that for privacy only children's first names and ages be provided in any reporting of children's views from the consultations.

In consultations such as these, participation itself demonstrates to children that they are valued citizens. In order to foster mutual respect, then, it was important for the children's participation to be voluntary and for children to be invited rather than expected to participate in the consultations. It was suggested that educators provide children with a formal invitation to demonstrate choice and respect. A template that could be adapted was provided as illustrated in Figure 3.3. It was suggested that such an invitation could be provided to each child or used as a flyer. Educators co-ordinating the consultations were encouraged to explain to children, particularly those that were unable to read, what the invitation said and what activities the children might be involved with and how the information children were to provide would be used to shape their communities.

Post-induction professional development

Following the induction workshop, participants needed to continue shaping their ideas and put them into practice in their sites. This involved co-operative planning with colleagues and peers to optimise success of the consultation process and provide additional opportunities for professional development through further reflection and sharing of ideas. As not all educators facilitating the consultations attended the induction workshop, those in attendance shared information and discussed ideas back at their sites.

Establishing and strengthening connections with peers outside of the immediate work team, such as other sites involved with similar consultations, also came into play. So doing expanded the sharing of information and ideas and provided opportunities to seek independent input from other sources.

Educators at the workshop also explored how children themselves could contribute to the professional development process and what could be learned through their contributions. Chapter 10 provides some insightful observations

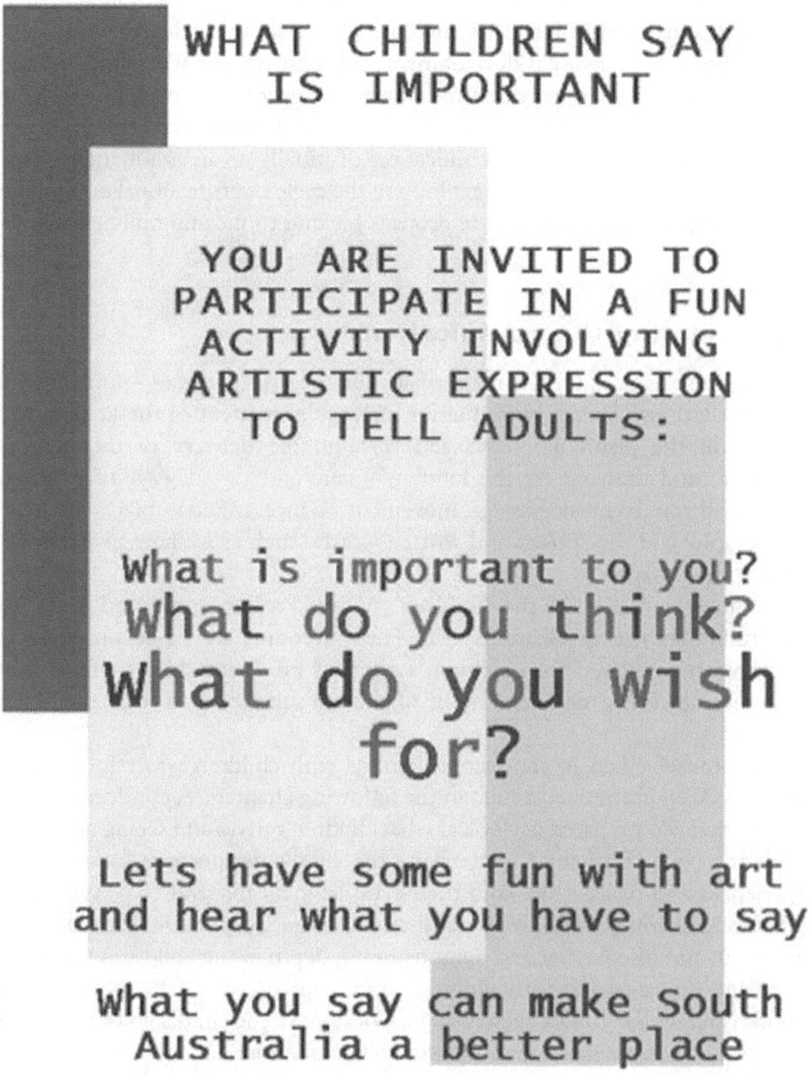

WHAT CHILDREN SAY IS IMPORTANT

YOU ARE INVITED TO PARTICIPATE IN A FUN ACTIVITY INVOLVING ARTISTIC EXPRESSION TO TELL ADULTS:

What is important to you?
What do you think?
What do you wish for?

Lets have some fun with art and hear what you have to say

What you say can make South Australia a better place

Figure 3.3 A sample invitation

from educators in terms of what they learned from children throughout the Children's Voices Project.

As a final stage in the first loop of the cycle of professional development outlined in Figure 3.2, a post-project workshop was held to bring together partners and participants to share their experiences and complete the learning journey cycle associated with the project, while recognising the continuous nature of learning and development. Again self-reflection was valuable at this workshop, and so was the opportunity taken to celebrate achievements.

In addition to individual development, the post-project workshop enhanced the collective learning of participants in order to improve and maximise outcomes achievable in future children's voices projects and practices. The sharing and celebrating of successes and identification of pitfalls or areas for improvement were valuable in informing the next loop of the cycle of professional development that would commence with future projects seeking to meaningfully engage with children.

Implementing the consultations

At last came the time for the proverbial rubber to hit the road – implementing the consultations. This implementation saw the enactment of the key principles outlined in the planning phases and through the delivery of the induction workshop; and drawing on the kinds of many and varied ways of expressing meaning through music, song, movement, dance, drama, play, visual arts, photography and the spoken and written word – such as we have also described earlier in this chapter.

The implementation of the Children's Voices Project is explored in the four case studies set out in Chapters 4–7. These accounts are based on educators' interviews triangulated with children's artefacts produced during the consultations and educators' documentation of the consultations through their words and photos.

The mindset taken in these consultations with children was critical to their success, as seen in the case studies in the following chapters. A conducive mindset was one that was prepared to: look at what children can do and seeing and making visible the competent child; understand the child's perspectives by seeing their experiences and realities through their eyes; have meaningful conversation with and among children through give-and-take dialogue; explore with children what they mean and discovering and demonstrating depth in the child's meaning; step back from doing to and for children and instead co-construct experiences with children and let the child's agency do its work; make the child's voice audible and their insights visible through authentic documentation; and sustain engagement with the child over time – for, as one educator succinctly put it, if we don't do these consultations well, when will we have the time to do them over?

Chapter 4

Children make their voices visible through visual arts in Limestone Town

The flowers are important.

(Graham, age four)

This case study describes how two- to four-year-old children in a kindergarten and rural care service engaged in the consultations through visual arts over a seven-week period. This case study highlights how such engagement occurs in a community of practice – practice in which children develop their tools of engagement, founded on observing children closely and having a deep awareness of children, documenting and listening to what children express. In this community of practice, the competent child shone through – their minds taken seriously, their oral and visual literacies for expressing meaning further honed – and in this, so too did the competent educator shine. This case study brings into clear focus the power of taking young children's minds seriously, showcasing their capacity for sustained attention and somewhat technical conversation about abstract ideas.

Contextual information

This case study focuses on consultations conducted with children and educators at services we call Limestone Town Kindergarten and Limestone Town Rural Care. At the time of the consultations, Limestone Town and its outlying areas had a population of 2,200 people and was geographically isolated from major centres. Situated in a rural region with a relatively young population, agriculture, forestry, fishing, manufacturing and a wine industry dominated the local workforce. There was a variable range of income levels. Leisure activities included beach, boat and jetty fishing, sailing, diving, golf, bowls, tennis and beach swimming.

At the time of the study, Limestone Town Kindergarten was a community hub for the district. The Kindergarten had an enrolment of 22 children, 27 per cent of whom travelled from outlying rural areas; 27 per cent had what was called 'oral language issues'; 13 per cent were on the preschool support programme, supporting children with additional needs; and 4.5 per cent spoke languages in addition to/other than English at home. A sizeable proportion of families were living in low socio-economic circumstances.

Also at the time of the study, Limestone Town Rural Care was a fully accredited centre-based long day care service. The service operated from 8.00 am to 6.00 pm Monday to Friday. While it was offered for children aged six weeks to twelve years, the children attending during the course of this study were aged between one and five years. There were twenty-two children enrolled in the service, with an average of four children attending every day.

Parents were encouraged to be involved in the centre in various ways, including remaining in the centre after drop-off to work with their children, running weekly play groups and being actively involved in the Governing Council.

Framing purpose and problem for engagement

Educators at the Limestone Town Kindergarten and Rural Care services met and developed what they called 'an inquiry approach' to plan, implement and document the consultations with their children – retaining the broad thematic focus of the consultations on what is important to children in their communities and what do children wish for in their lives. The questions educators asked of themselves to reflectively guide their planning processes were:

- How might we explore the consultation theme in a meaningful way with children?
- How might we document children's voices respectfully?
- What might be the challenges to eliciting children's authentic ideas and thoughts?
- How can we make children's thinking visible to others?
- How confident do we feel about our capacity to consult with children?
- Where might we begin?
- What resources and support might we need?
- What documentation will we need to collect and how?
- How can we best utilise financial resources?

In terms of the first question, the educators decided they would start by having a general discussion with the children about what was important to them in their communities, in terms of the places, people and activities they experience and enjoy.

Following this general discussion, educators planned to further explore such questions in dialogue with children on a one-to-one basis. The questions they planned for these individual conversations were:

- Where are the places you go in Limestone Town? Where are the places you like and why?
- What activities do you like doing at these places?
- How do you feel when you are doing these activities?
- Who do you like to spend time with at these places?

Visual arts in Limestone Town 49

- How do you feel when you are at these places with these people?
- What things do you like seeing or doing at these places?
- What things would you like to see and do that you have never done before?
- Are there any places you do not like to visit?
- Are there any activities that you do not like to do?

If, after these conversations, educators sought more information from a child, they would note that on that child's recording sheet. As for the educators' next planning question related to respectfully documenting children's voices, they identified the need to be transparent with children about how they would record what children said, and be explicit with children in terms of valuing their views.

As the educators anticipated challenges to eliciting children's authentic views, they focused on how to do so with children who were, as they described, 'non-verbal due to their additional needs'. In the discussion that ensued, educators affirmed their roles as researchers of and with their children. As documented in their planning material:

> Staff decided to carefully observe and listen to these children throughout this project. We would watch what the children enjoyed doing at the kindergarten and rural care, as well as use our knowledge of that child, our observations, photos and work samples. We would also enlist the help of the parents and ask them what their child likes doing and places they like to visit. We felt by doing this, we would be able to create the child's own voice.

Educators planned to make children's thinking visible through the documentation of their individual conversations with children, children's draft pictures and final artworks, and recording what children said as they painted.

In terms of reflecting on their own confidence and capacity to authentically consult with young children, educators acknowledged their professional engagement with young children in the preschool and childcare sector over many years and across diverse settings and circumstances. Educators viewed their staff stability as an enabling factor, as Kelly explained:

> We've probably been together for two years. We haven't had a staff change for two years, which is actually good. I think having that stability is really important because then you can actually really get in and look deeply.

Educators also acknowledged the focus they had taken to date with tuning into children's views:

> We have been asking children to tell us about their knowledge of certain topics, or tell us a story consistently throughout the child's time at preschool, as part of developing children's oral literacy, which is a site priority. We have also consistently recorded children's language and stories by scribing.

50 Visual arts in Limestone Town

Deciding where to begin, educators discussed how to give parents and children general information about the consultations. They took the matter to the governing council and talked about the central theme of the consultations and the strategy and approach they would take. The parent council took strong interest and suggested artists in the community with whom they might work.

There was, however, some concern about young children's involvement. As the centre's director, whom we call Kelly, explained in an interview, the council was 'concerned with the children's ability to understand what they like and don't like about Limestone Town, and about how we were going to do the questioning, not just about listening'. Staff reassured the council about the various questioning techniques they had planned to use with children, supported by cross-checks with families and their own observations and knowledge of children.

From that point and with the council's agreement, letters were sent home to children and parents, inviting them to participate in the consultations, accompanied by consent forms and a description of the consultations:

> Staff also spoke to parents individually about the project, as we have a number of parents who don't have good literacy skills. So we had everybody on board which was absolutely marvellous. All parents were excited about it. There was no one saying: 'No, they can't be a part of it.' That was terrific.

The consultations were planned for a seven-week period as follows:

1. Whole group discussions with children in weeks one and two, accompanied by photos of the community taken at a young child's eye-level.
2. Individual conversations with children in weeks two, three and four about places, people and activities in their community, framed by the questions previously identified for these conversations.
3. Two local artists visiting the centre and talking with children about their artwork. Children use photos of their community as a visual reference as they develop and draft their artworks showing what they like and dislike about Limestone Town, supported as required by the visiting artists and centre staff.
4. Children work with centre staff to develop their final artworks, to be completed by week seven.

Resources and support that the educators required included digital cameras for photographing children's engagement throughout the consultations; art materials and stationery supplies; local artists; additional staffing and parent and volunteer helpers; voice recorders and a flip camera; and project support from DECS Head Office (including $1,000 allocated budget and professional advice and feedback as required).

How the encounter unfolded

Transparency and shared understanding about the purpose of the consultations were key principles planned at the outset and implemented throughout this encounter. As planned, educators initially had a general discussion with the children about what was important to them in their communities. This discussion was followed by individual conversations with each child, using the same questions for each child that the educators had planned 'to maintain a consistency throughout'. Educators explained to each child that they 'would be writing down what they said, as this was a really important thing they were telling us'. So it was that educators scribed what children said:

> We read [what children said] over and over again as a staff to hear what was important to the children . . . We wanted to make absolutely sure that we were true to the child and their voice . . . We then went to the parents and shared the survey with the parents. It was really exciting to have that confirmation from parents that we were spot-on – they verified children's likes and dislikes.

Educators sustained this dialogue with children with a varied range of language resources, and scaffolded children's participation accordingly. This scaffolding was founded on knowledge of the children and tuning into their ideas. For example:

> Some of the children may not have had some ideas about what they were going to do. I talked to one child about what he liked, and suggested that he bring in things that he liked. He talked about his Grandmas' garden. I asked him, 'Can you bring some of the leaves and some of the flowers that grandma has in her garden?' He brought them in and we talked more about that. So yes, sometimes we prompted children with ideas on their theme that they'd talked about.

Following these conversations, children prepared to engage in expressing their views of their local communities through painting. Children and educators worked with two artists in the local community – one an acrylic painter whom we call Pamela, the other an oils artist we call Lillian. These artists worked with children to develop children's conceptual and procedural tools of engagement in the consultations through visual arts. In the children's interactions that ensued with the artists, the educators felt it was very important to the authenticity of the consultations that the artists were 'not to have total control'. Thus children led the experience in terms of their choices about how to engage and what they wanted to paint to express their views about their local communities.

The acrylic artist, Pamela, brought her paintings with her on her visit to the centre. Included were two paintings of her son that she was currently working

52 Visual arts in Limestone Town

on. Pamela spoke about getting an idea for one of these paintings from a photo of her son climbing a tree. She also spoke about the influence that a children's book about a child climbing a tree had on her painting.

Pamela shared her painting techniques with the children. She explained how she began with light colours, then gradually added darker ones. She showed the children sketchbooks of her drawings, colour-mixing experiments, and bits and pieces such as fabric samples and leaf prints. Pamela also spoke about how early modern artists painted light and dark shades, and shared a painting by Paul Cézanne that was also influencing her artwork. She demonstrated the tools of her trade – her brushes, paints, easel and painting smock.

Pamela set her easel up in a corner and painted throughout the morning, further arousing children's curiosity. Some children went up and looked at what she was doing, others were more reluctant and kept their distance. Others went up and questioned Pamela about her being there and her painting.

Pamela later shared a painting of a surf fisherman that she had completed. Children were intrigued by the waves and wondered how she had painted them, and so Pamela demonstrated her paint-flicking technique.

This painting sparked children's interest in the sea and so a focus on the sea was the direction this encounter next took. Educators made up various shades of blue and white, and used local photos they had taken of the sea for children's visual reference. As well, children could see the ocean from their window in the centre. Pamela worked with small groups of children, talking with them about the colours of the sea and movement of the waves.

They also talked about movement from observing and being on swings in the playground, and talked about language used to describe movement – for example, 'slower' and 'faster' in terms of speed, and 'higher' and 'lower' in terms of spatial relationships.

Children began to paint their ideas on large sheets of paper on an easel or the floor. They freely experimented with colours and techniques to create different light and movement effects and to portray what they wished to express. Children enthusiastically attempted Pamela's paint-flicking technique, many using this technique in their final artworks.

On Pamela's second visit, she brought in other photos and pieces of art. One shot was of her daughter jumping in the air. Pamela explained to the children that her daughter 'looks like she is frozen. It's a bit blurry. You can see a bit of her arm where her leg was' because her body was shifting. Talk continued about how Pamela captures movement in dance, including a small quilt she had crafted from sewing together six images of a dancer in motion.

Children also pored over a book of modern art, with particular attention given to Toulouse-Lautrec's painting of a walking dog to talk about movement of the dog's legs. They also looked at a photo of James Morrison playing his trumpet, and talked about the movement of music going round and round. This photo led to the provocation, 'How would I paint that sound? What would that music look like?'

Visual arts in Limestone Town 53

Pamela worked with children in small groups, talking about experiences like being on a swing, riding a skateboard and making wheels on a bike turn around. The children were very enthusiastic in wanting to continue to experiment with movement in their paintings, and so they did with intent absorption and quiet reflection, as evidenced in the photos taken of the experience. Following this discussion, Pamela worked with the children as they experimented with capturing movement in their own paintings. Children painted pictures of the park, depicting movement in the wheels of a bike, the motion of a swing, the running of a child, the rolling of a skateboard at the local skate park.

Another artist was also involved – Lillian, who specialised in oil paintings of historic buildings, landscapes and seascapes. She also brought in a range of her paintings to share and talk about with the children. Many of her paintings were about her family history – buildings in which family members had lived, the coastline where her ancestors had been shipwrecked, and land her family owned.

Lillian talked about how she starts a painting. She explained that because oils take a long time to dry, she paints from photos. She described her process where she paints or draws what she is going to do, then begins usually by painting the sky. She also talked about the tools of her trade, including her tubes of paint, her paint palette, the trowel she uses to mix her paints, and the brushes and palette knife with which she paints.

Given children's interest in parks, Lillian worked with children in small groups to paint their local parks. They talked about the colours and shapes of playground equipment there. Children then moved on to develop drafts of their own paintings of playgrounds and skate parks, and as with Pamela, experiment with their techniques.

In these different encounters where children experimented with techniques and drafted their ideas, children were encouraged to 'have a go' and their paintings were respected and appreciated. As children's ideas and processes took hold with greater mastery and confidence, the artists and educators stepped back from the child, ever-watchful and ready to assist as needed.

The engagement between children and the two artists was founded on recognition of children's own expert minds and ways of meaning – it took children's minds very seriously indeed. Being taken seriously saw the children of their own accord sustain their engagement in these conversations for forty minutes at a stretch – challenging preconceived notions about children's capacity for attention and abstract talk. As Kelly observed: 'You know, it was absolutely stunning, because it was all sort of inquiry – "how do I do this?" It was really engaging to the children.'

In this talk, too, artists' and children's personal experiences and interests were foregrounded. What inspired and influenced the artists entwined with the inspiration and influences that children saw in their local community.

From these influences and inspiration, children began to create their final artworks for the consultations. In preparation, educators returned to the individual conversations they had had with children at the outset of this encounter, in which children had spoken about people, places and activities in their community. Educators revisited the written recording of each child's conversation with that child, and asked the child on that basis to think about a painting he or she would like to create to express his or her views in whatever medium he or she chose. Children created their final artworks in oils or acrylics, using collage to embellish their paintings. Educators scribed the oral texts that the children composed about their paintings.

Structures and modes that sustained dialogue

At the outset of these consultations, Limestone Town educators expressed their concern with oral literacy issues among 27 per cent of their children. The visual arts modes used in this encounter addressed this concern at two levels – these modes, accompanied by in-depth dialogue and hands-on exploration, in meaningful whole group, small group and individual situations, enabled children to effectively participate in the consultations and exercise their citizenship, while further enriching children's oral and visual literacies alike. Such enrichment enabled children to more fully express their views for the purposes of the consultations, as we'll later see when exploring their themes later in this chapter. As evidenced in the educators' observational records, 'children developed language around art terminology. There was very rich learning here.' Some children also used photos. For example, an autistic boy took photos of what he liked doing at the centre and home, and incorporated these images into his painting.

A key structural challenge that educators found they needed to work with to make this an effective encounter was time:

> Time was the biggest thing for us, we had to be mindful about time. We would have liked to have done some of the Rural Care Group, with some of the younger children. Trying to get down the children's ideas about their paintings, that was probably the hardest thing, considering that we are only two days a week. The two-year-olds did paintings of the beach. We just let them lead the way and we would have liked to have gone deeper with this with more time (before handing in the final report to DECS).

Working with these time constraints, educators also were concerned about how they recorded what children said during this encounter:

> We were unable to audio-record what the children were saying and what they answered. That was probably the hardest thing while running the programme at the same time, and the interruptions. We did not do an audio-recording of what the children were saying while they were painting. My teacher actually did have a couple of voice recorders that we could plug into the computer and we did – that took time to get those, and we were

only able to use those with the last visit. My teacher was able to get those and I was able to put those into my documentation. It would have been handy to actually have those little voice recorders because you can sit them down and they pick up the voices quite well, and then they just plug into the computer.

Also coming to light in these experiences was an appreciation of broader network and collegial structures that enable or constrain dialogue among educators to support and enrich, inform and shape their work:

> When we did this project, I thought, 'Oh, OK, who am I going to talk to?' For once there wasn't anyone else doing what we were about to do. It probably would have been nice to have got on the phone to others involved in the consultations at other sites and hear what they were doing. Maybe we might have been able to take on board some of the things that other people might have been doing. Perhaps there could have been a chat line or something like that.

These constraints were counter-balanced to some degree by the educators' sense of their own staff stability:

> I just really hope that we all stay together. You know, it takes a few years to get that happening. We've probably been together for two years. We haven't had a staff change for two years, which is actually good. I think having that stability is really important because then you can really get in and look deeply into things with children and what we do in our programs.

These constraints notwithstanding, educators found the consultations to be a transforming experience in terms of how they listen to children:

> There's been a change in thinking about how we listen to what children say. There's a great respect, I think it's a very powerful thing listening to children . . . It's a very, very powerful thing . . . If you really listen, it's amazing what children know and what children can do. I think it's really, really important for us to actually listen. I think this project has really proved that really.

Children's themes

What follows is an account of the themes that emerged from children's conversations, paintings and oral text that their educators scribed. Each child produced quite an extended scribed text (ranging from a half to a full A4 page of single-space twelve-point font per child) – a tribute to the enriched language

56 Visual arts in Limestone Town

proficiencies of these children and their educators' and artists' scaffolding of same. We use extracts only from these extended texts to illustrate each thematic category.

Spending time at the beach

A frequent theme that emerged related to spending time at the beach with family and friends, playing in the sand and the ocean, and finding things such as shells, crabs, seaweed and seagulls. For example:

> I go to the beach with Nanny and Mummy . . . I like the beach because of dead crabs. But if you find real ones, they would snap you. They bury sand so they can live in there. My Mum just picks up the crabs and shows me. No, not real ones, just dead crabs.
>
> (Tyler, age 4)

> I like going to the beach . . . I build sandcastles with a bucket and shovel. I put shells and seaweed on. I go walking with Mummy on the beach. I find shells, little shells. I don't see crabs. I ride Daddy's bike, but not all by myself. I sit next to the handles. We ride on the beach. It feels good. It feels really fast. The seagulls fly away. Sometimes we have a picnic on the beach . . . Edward and I make a sandcastle. We tip the water over and the water goes away. It goes under the sand. I see little fish sometimes. We try to catch them but they swim away. We don't have a net.
>
> (Shauna, age 4)

> We like to build sandcastles. Steven gets the sand in the bucket and I get the water. Steven fills the bucket up with sand and I wet it down . . . I wear bathers and I take my teacup set. I fill it up with water and Steven drinks it. It is seawater and Steven spits it out. I pretend it's rainwater but it's actually seawater. Sometimes I get an ice-cream, it cools me down from the hot sun.
>
> (Penny, age 4)

> [The beach] has got shells and I really want Travis, Wendy, Kate and Tony's brothers to feed the seal. It's got flippers and it's a baby. It jumps up to get the fish. One day Kale went to go and get some bag of fish for the seal, and the seal was coming up to Kale.
>
> (Martin, age 4)

Playing in the sea

Another theme closely related to spending time at the beach was actually playing in the sea with family and friends. This theme included swimming in the water, going to the boat ramp, going fishing in a boat, and going to the jetty and the lighthouse. For example:

> I go in Poppy's swimming pool. I just put my toes in the beach. I just like cold water and hot and warm water. Aunty Mary gave me a surf board.
>
> (Tyler, age 4)

> Steven likes to play in the water with me. We like to jump over the waves. You go in the water and you find a little wave and then you jump over it . . . We have a picnic on the boat – fritters, salad and soup. I like soup. We fish. Steven and me don't know how to put everything on [the fishing line] but Daddy does. He puts the bait on first, then he puts the hook and then he throws it in the water. I catched a bit of seaweed and Steven catched a fish. Steven just goes over little waves with his kickboard. I push myself on the waves. I go a bit far . . . The white stuff in the water looks like snow. I like to try and catch the white snow water.
>
> (Penny, age 4)

> Natasha be all scared of going fast. I am brave. I like to go fast on the boat. One day my Dad said I can go fishing with him on the boat all by myself, just my Dad and me. We haven't done it yet, but one day we will. Well, I like squid, we turn it into calamari. I like going fast in the water and I scream because I like it. When we go fast, a bit of the water goes up and the other bit goes down. One day when we went fast, Natasha got scared and she cried, but I didn't . . . I like getting fish to have for tea. I help to cook nuggets at home . . . One day we saw a seal poke its head up and one day we saw a dolphin jumping out of the water . . . We have our lifties on so we don't get water on us. We have craypots. We caught a different fish in the craypot. We used it for some more bait. Daddy goes out in the boat at night time for a couple of nights. Our boat is white and big . . . I am Dad's new fisherman.
>
> (Pippa, age 4)

> I like to go to the boat ramp. I like going fishing with my Pop . . . We go fishing with the boat and catch salmon and big sting sharks, they are about that little and we catch them and take them home and eat them. I like cleaning the boat with a pressure cleaner. You gotta put a hose onto the cleaner and the water comes again into an old bottle. There's a big long button and then, when you press it, all the water comes out. It's really poisonous . . . Last year when they got Dad's boat out of the water, the trailer got bogged in the water. Well all the men had to help, one had to drive, one had to push.
>
> (Owen, age 4)

58 Visual arts in Limestone Town

I swim in the water with my surfboard. We collect shells. I collect them with Mum and Rebecca.

(Opal, age 4)

We go fishing in my brand new boat and I buyed it from a man's house. Dad catched a shark, he didn't go out right deep, just near the shallow . . . Sometimes Dad and me and Mum and Violet go out. Sometimes dolphins go near Pop's boat and sometimes they go near our boat. Nanna spotted a dolphin in my brand new boat when we were giving it a test. Oh yeah, I saw a seal on the beach, a dead one washed up and it was stinky . . . I might be a Cray when I grow up.

(Oscar, age 4)

Actually I fish off the jetty where it is far out near the granites. You can't fish when there's seaweed because you catch the seaweed, but you can catch fish where you put your boats in at Limestone Town. There is no seaweed there, sometimes, but only one bit.

(Nick, age 4)

I like going fishing and swimming. I like to go swimming with Travis, with his brothers and Wendy and Kate and Michael my brother. I dig a big hole in the water and I sit in it. It was really deep. I dig forever and I got out when it was time to go.

(Martin, age 4)

Going to the park

Going to the park with family and friends emerged as a strong theme, too, among these Limestone Town children. Playing in the playground, having picnics, enjoying nature, seeing fireworks at night, going to the skate park, riding bikes on the bike track, all figured prominently in this category – even the local rubbish dump rated a mention as a different kind of playground. For example:

When me and my mummy and daddy and everyone else went to the park and watched the fireworks, some were going up and BOOM! And the others were doing that too. It looked fantastic. I love pink, purple and white . . . I've never seen fireworks before. I saw them at the night time. I said, 'Mummy and Daddy, when can I see the fireworks?' And they said, 'Night time.' I did say that too many times. They had a headache. Daddy didn't hear me, so he didn't get a headache. I want to see the fireworks again. It doesn't scare me at all.

(Wendy, age 4)

Visual arts in Limestone Town 59

You get to do tricks when you go up the ramp [at the skate park]. You just do whatever you want – skateboard ones, rip stick ones and scooter ones. I like to do skate board ones . . . The skate park is like, ramps. I reckon it's made of glitter and ramps. I see my brothers go there and Paul and Tony. I like to do tricks. Wade was at the party and showed me how to do the tricks. You ride first, and then you push your scooter off, that's my trick. I think four people go there. It's, like, near the fixing shops. It takes me 40 hours to get there. I ride my bike and scooter around the house . . . I want to do back flips. You go up the ramp really high. You can do turning-around tricks. Mum says, 'Be careful,' and I say, 'I am careful.'

(Travis, age 4)

I love to ride my bike at home and I love to ride my bike down the street, but sometimes my mum says 'No'. It feels like I'm happy. I love to go to the playground on my bike. I put my bike in the playground near the table.

(Opal, age 4)

I like going to the garbage dump with Daddy because I like throwing stuff off the Ute into the garbage dump. It makes me laugh when I always see the garbage dump. Sometimes we see our friends from across us. Sometimes we take nappy boxes, old house bits and wood. When I throw it off, it makes a thunder noise. Sometimes we see old trucks and old cars and we see old beach chairs. I like climbing up the garbage sometimes with my friend and sometimes I climb up there by myself. I don't like the garbage dump because it's smelly and yucky.

(Nick, age 4)

I just want to play on the swings. I like to go up and high. It feels good because I like fun. I like to go with Helen and Sharon and Gerry. These are all the twirly things and they're giving you a swing . . . I go to the biggest park 'cause that's my favourite . . . When I need to go to another big playground, there'll be a crash where there's a big thunder. I just got my gun right here so I can shoot the rain clouds. Mummy waits for 100 minutes.

(Lenny, age 4)

Eating out and buying food

Another area of thematic interest that arose among the children was eating out and buying food with family and friends – whether at the shops or the diner in the local petrol station, the bakery, the pub or the town's Big Lobster[1] (a seventeen-metre tall steel and fibre-glass sculpture of a lobster that houses

60 Visual arts in Limestone Town

a visitor's centre and restaurant and is affectionately known as Larry by the townsfolk). For example:

> I like to see Larry. I go there to eat something to eat. I like to eat fish and chips and drink lemonade. I go under Larry, it is dark. It's like a cave. Larry is really big. I go under with Yvette . . . He is spiky and he feels good . . . I go with Mummy and Daddy and Yvette and sometimes I go with my friends. Sometimes we have dinner. I have rice to eat. The fire at Larry's makes me warm. I go there on all sorts of days.
>
> (Zoe, age 4)

> I go to ice-cream shops. I like the rainbow ones. Do you know what my favourite colour is? Green!
>
> (Tyler, age 4)

Visiting extended family and friends

A significant thread running throughout these themes, as so far seen, was family and friends. It is no surprise then, that another category of interest for children was visiting extended family and friends. Such visits included helping in the garden, sleeping over, seeing nature, and going to family members' workplaces, be it a farm, a fishing boat or the local shops. For example:

> Nanna's garden is big and it's fluffy and white. It has Christmas birds that scare all the birds away and it flaps. I have a little pumpkin. It is growing. It will take two months to grow or maybe one month. I play throwing and I have a wheelbarrow and shovel . . . We did actually dig and make holes and try to fill the hole in that I dug last night. I like my motor bike but I don't ride it at Grandma's garden because it will squish the plants . . . I share my pumpkin with my nan and Dad and Mum and George. It's going to be big, like this many, and then I will draw on it a face, and we put a glow thing in it to light it up and go in a competition. Flowers are beautiful and shiny in Grandma's garden. The yellow is Grandma's favourite, they are way down the back, they grow on the tree actually. I saw some bees up in Grandma's greenhouse. They were doing bad stuff. They were making honey for us.
>
> (Eddie, age 4)

Enjoying nature

Be it in the gardens of families, friends and relations, or at local parks and beaches, or further afield, a love of nature figured prominently among these Limestone Town children's thematic interests. For example:

The flowers are important because we've got flowers growing on our road and in our yard and driveway.

(Graham, age 4)

I like butterflies and wrens. I see them every day and every night. I have a bird eater for them. We put bird-seed on it and we put peanut butter on it so the bird-seed sticks to it. And I see a rainbow. I like rainbows. All of them are my favourite colours. I hang the bird eater on my backyard tree every night. Every day when it's breakfast they come out to eat. Nanny Barb has a bird eater too. She has a pet bird called Bird. Poppy makes the eaters . . . I take the bird feeder off our tree and take it to the park and hold it. Then the birds come up to it. It makes me feel good. They sometimes bite my finger, because they've got very sharp beaks. Sometimes I cry when they do that . . . Seagulls and magpies, they eat our chips at the park for lunch. I pat them and they don't bite me. We hold our bird eater so that the birds can eat them. I love them so much.

(Quinn, age 4)

Well, I normally like horses. My dad normally rides them but that was ages ago. I like horses because they are so friendly and so big. They normally let us ride them but we don't have one, only at Terry's mother's farm . . . I like to see the horses with Dad and Mum. I love sheep and kangaroos. I always want to be a farmer. Farmers milk cows and put them in different yards.

(Graham, age 4)

I look at the sky and I see shapes in the clouds. Babies, horses and dragons and see-saws. It makes me want to climb up trees. I love to get to the clouds so I can see properly.

(Quinn, age 4)

Life on the farm was a compelling occupation for one child:

I like sweeping in the shed. We made the broom. The wool gets sold to the market and then it goes to the factory. Then you make socks out of it. There are shearer things that shear the sheep, the hand piece. Dad picks the wool up and he takes it to Mr Williams in Limestone Town. He takes it on Pa's truck . . . I sweep while the shearers shear . . . They work all day but when it's night time, they go home. Shearing sheep is easy. The wool feels soft . . . I like working with the sheep. Dad draughts them and I am playing. We have motor bikes to get the sheep in . . . I ride on the front. We have a farm and I like to help Dad.

(John, age 4)

62   Visual arts in Limestone Town

What children don't like

Finally, children expressed dislike for particular places and things, including seaweed, mosquitoes, and garbage and litter (including smelly bins and the dump). For example:

> I don't like seaweed when there is lots. It's yucky 'cause it's black. When there is lots of seaweed, we park in a safe spot and we walk. We find little white things in the seaweed, the pop things.
>
> (Shauna, age 4)

> I like the jetty because there is water to play. There is lots of seaweed. I don't like the seaweed because it's yucky, so it smells yucky.
>
> (Oscar, age 4)

> I don't like it when the seagulls got my doughnut at the park. I got the doughnut at the bakery. I felt upset that the seagull took my doughnut.
>
> (Wendy, age 4)

> The park is near a pub. The pub I don't like because it takes too long to get home.
>
> (Wendy, age 4)

> Seaweed sticks to your feet when you go in the water. It feels yucky. I try to wash my feet, but water didn't work at the beach. When we went to Grant's, Grant washed the seaweed off with a hose. That worked.
>
> (Anthony, age 4)

> [I don't want to visit] an island if there were pirates. Pirates are very, very scary.
>
> (Quinn, age 4)

> I don't like the seaweed because there is brown water . . . and it stinks because it's been in the water . . . and there is sand on it and water in it. It looks like big piles of black sand and we can't get in. When they've got it all piled up, a big truck comes and picks it up. Actually, 200 trucks come. Then there is no seaweed. It makes me feel happy. Seaweed makes me feel yucky.
>
> (Matthew, age 4)

> I don't like litter. When I see litter, it makes me mad and then I go into Hulk. I see litter when they throw it around, and I feel like throwing them in the bin. It's not good to litter because it's always mean. You might slip over and fall down and hurt your head. When I'm Hulk, I pick the rubbish

Visual arts in Limestone Town 63

up and put it in the bin. I see chip rubbish and fruity bar rubbish and lolly rubbish. I see rubbish everywhere, but not at kindy, because kindy always has to stay clean. Sometimes all the other people try to throw their rubbish in the bin, but it doesn't go in. Not me, I don't do that. I am the only one that goes up to the bin and drops the rubbish in. Sometimes when the rubbish is empty, it doesn't go in the bin because it doesn't fly very well when it doesn't have anything in it. But a paper plane can fly better without anything in it . . . Litter is bad, so put it in the bin.

(Jason, age 4)

When all was said and done and painted in this encounter, Limestone Town Kindergarten and Rural Care held a special night that displayed children's works. This event gave parents and community members an important opportunity to see the children's creations and hear their words about what mattered to them in their local community lives.

Reflecting on the Limestone Town case study

Taking children's minds seriously and acknowledging and respecting their great capacity to share their views in dialogic encounters with others clearly empowered children to engage in these consultations. Educators and families put aside their preconceptions about young children's limitations – whether these preconceptions were age-related, language-related or related to notions about children's capacity for abstract thinking, technical talk or prolonged engagement. In so doing, children's pedagogic space was transformed. So, too, was the thinking of those who witnessed and supported children's engagement:

We were blown away by the wonderful sense of hope of one of the respondents. We asked, 'What do you hope for?' 'What would you like to do?' One thing was that she wanted to be a fairy, and her comment was she wanted to be a doctor when she grew up. I can't remember the exact words but it was something like 'reach for the stars'. The optimism in these children was really amazing. There was passion in children's voices about what they liked or didn't like . . . what was important to children flowed really easily . . . One of the parents was shocked their child was not interested in football but skateboarding instead. They didn't know that. It was confronting but they accepted that.

This observed hope and optimism in children strongly resonates with Freire's emphasis (1983) on hope that imbues authentic and sustainable dialogic encounters – the same ideal that mobilises participants to express their vision for their world, and more, ways to realise that vision. For, as Friere (1983, p. 80) reminds us, 'if the dialoguers expect nothing to come of their efforts, their encounter will be empty and sterile, bureaucratic and tedious'.

64 Visual arts in Limestone Town

Freire (1983, pp. 77–8) also has written:

> dialogue cannot exist . . . in the absence of a profound love for the world and for men. The naming of the world which is an act of creation and re-creation, is not possible if it is not infused with love.

In relating this ideal to the Limestone Town encounter, we call to mind the programme director's own reflection:

> I think we can underestimate the power of the under-fives. The children engaged really well and provided some really insightful responses. We could hear the children's voices – we could hear their passion.

Children's passion clearly was borne of their love for their local community worlds and the people with whom they shared it. While the children talked and painted about places and activities, it is the qualities of these experiences to which we must pay heed – the sense of adventure, the sense of connectedness to nature, the sense of exhilaration when one rides fast or swings high, the sense of being and doing with others, the sense of being in and with the world.

It is in children's rich portrayals of these experiences that we live again the spirit of childhood. It is that spirit that needs to imbue decision-making processes about child-friendly spaces as much as the details that children lovingly describe in their inimitable, highly contextualised and idiosyncratic ways.

Note

1. The Big Lobster is a seventeen-metre tall steel and fibre-glass sculpture of a lobster that houses a visitor's centre and restaurant. It is one of 'Australia's Big Things', a collection of over-sized novelty architecture and sculptures located throughout the nation. The Big Lobster is affectionately known as 'Larry' by the local townsfolk.

Chapter 5

Children see themselves in a new frame through photography in an Eyre and Western community

That's me!

(Michael, age 4)

This case study tells a story of empowerment that comes from recognising the competent child – recognition that comes when adults move from a preoccupation with *what* children are (e.g. developmentally delayed, disabled, impaired) to *who* children are. When adults remove preconceived ceilings from children, as this case study highlights, the child's competence can shine through, allowing children to exercise their citizenship through modes they know best – play and an inquiring mind.

Contextual information

This case study was located in the Eyre and Western region, more specifically in a remote rural region with below average incomes and a predominance of farming and labouring occupations. The general level of education and qualifications in the community was below state average.

The site was a learning partnership programme conducted in children's homes for families with children aged birth to four years. The programme's purpose to support families' involvement in their children's learning through play. Families at whom the programme was targeted include those living in social or geographic isolation; families and their children experiencing mental health issues, disabilities or developmental delays; new arrivals to Australia; young parents; and families living in poverty. Indigenous families were given particular priority.

At the time of the study, the programme's educator, whom we call Nicola, visited families in their homes for very specific purposes, as she described:

> I do the home visits specifically to each family . . . Often the children are delayed or sometimes the parents are. Sometimes it's because the children are a long way out of towns and things like that. The program has a lot of children with disabilities in varying ranges and severities . . . Some of the

children have speech issues, that sort of thing. Sometimes the children have very severe disabilities, so it's a wide range.

The children who engaged in the consultations experienced a range of such issues that they surmounted with their families on a daily basis. These issues included autism, speech delays, language difficulties, sensory processing difficulties, hearing impairment, a severe heart condition that involved frequent periods in hospital, and schizencephaly, a condition that causes severe global developmental delay and frequent seizures.

Nicola talked about key considerations when inviting children and families to be involved in the consultations. She thought about families who would 'cope with the consultations' in terms of being able to 'let their children take the lead', observing that 'some of the families want to do everything for their children'. Another consideration concerned the children and how they, too, might 'cope' with being involved, in view of acknowledging the children's perceived 'disabilities or delays'.

Framing purpose and problem for engagement

As Nicola approached the consultations, she initially found herself being quite protective of families and children by being selective about whom she would include in the consultations and why:

> The first thing that I did was to think quite specifically about what families and what sort of families I would offer this to. I have 38 families on my books all over the peninsula. I needed to think number one, 'What families would cope with it?' Families that would be able to let their children do it. Some of my families want to do everything for their children. Then I had to think about, 'OK, can this child cope with this?' I had to really think about the children themselves, because every child I have got, every child I have got disabilities or delays of some sort. I didn't want it to be a failure, something they couldn't cope with. So I had to think quite hard about who I would offer it to.

These initial deliberations were framed by a desire for children's agency to be unfettered to do its work by supporting their engagement in ways they could succeed – as Nicola put it, 'making a choice that the children were to be in control . . . and not have others do the work for them':

> I had to be mindful of how was I going to travel out of Eyre Town. The parents were very good with regards to the actual work with the consent forms. They were really, really good about that, which was excellent. There were no issues. Parents were very open about that, I was pleased about that.

Children and their educators and families used digital photography and information technology as its core strategy over a four-week period. Children were provided with digital cameras with which they took photos in their local community to show what they liked and didn't like, and to act as springboards for conversations with children about their views of their community.

What Nicola also believed important in setting up this experience was 'giving children a reason to engage' and time to explore the cameras. She was aware that many of these children did not have prior experience with cameras, and some families did not own a camera. Highlighted here is the need to be careful about assumptions we make about resources to which children do and do not have access, related to the digital divide in our society that is well documented in the research literature. What initially was seen to be a potential problem or limitation transformed into opportunity and provocation, as we see unfold in the dialogic encounters that occurred.

Nicola sent an invitation to children and families to participate. The invitation was headed, 'What children say is important', and worded as follows:

> Listening to children through photography.
> You and your child are invited to be part of the consultation with children for the new South Australian State Plan. Your family will be given a digital camera and memory card that you get to keep, and asked to take photos to help us understand more about what is important to children. We want to know: What is important to children? What do children wish for? If your family would like to be involved, please let me know as soon as possible.

Nicola then sent a further letter to families who gave their consent for their children and themselves to be involved, headed with the focal question she had framed:

> What do children care about in their community?
> Thank you for agreeing to be part of this exciting project. Your child will be contributing to the next State Strategic Plan through their photos of what is important to them.
> We are giving your child and family a camera and memory card that you will be able to keep as a thank you for being part of the project.
> We think there are lots of places, people and activities that are part of your child's life that are very important to them. Through your child taking photos of these special things, we will be hearing the stories about why they matter so much.
> Some of the areas we think might be important are:
>
> * Home – both inside and outside
> * People – both family and those further afield

68 Photography in an Eyre and Western community

- Activities
- Places.

But your child might have some other ideas! Start with taking one of these areas, such as inside your home, and talk about what your child likes to do there, and what their favourite things are. For example, they might really like a particular room, or love watching TV with their brother. Let them take lots of pictures of what they really like. They will get a chance to choose their very favourite photos later.

Some questions might be:

- What are your favourite things inside the house?
- What do you like doing inside?
- Where do you like playing?
- Who are your favourite people?

Repeat this for outside at home, for the people they care about, for all the things they like to do, and the places they like best.

Intended to provide a scaffold, Nicola developed these suggestions further as a web of possibilities. At the heart of the web was the question, 'What matters to your child?' Surrounding this central question were contributing questions that provided slightly different angles for parents to explore with their children:

- What makes your child smile or laugh?
- What makes your child feel happy?
- What are your child's favourite things?
- What is enjoyable to your child?

How the encounter unfolded

Educators worked collaboratively with parents and observed and documented children's engagement from exploring how to use the digital cameras to taking photos and talking about these. The encounter was a co-construction that followed children's leads.

Children engaged as competent decision-makers and decision-informers, empowered by the actions families and educators took to foster children's agency and participation. Witnessing children's competent participation led their families and educators to re-frame their views of their children. This re-framing grew out of the dialogic encounter and adults stepped back and allowed themselves to be guided by the children. They gave children 'control and choices about what they do'. As importantly, they gave children time to explore, experiment, observe, discover and become familiar with the camera before putting it to work for the consultations. All the while, educators and families discerningly watched and actively listened to the children, tuning into their verbal and non-verbal communication cues. Adults assisted as required. As described by Nicola:

> Working with the children meant they were in control of what photographs they decided to take and how they independently used the camera – unless they needed help, then we'd help and show them. There were always new photographs that the children were taking when I went back. I don't think we really needed to change anything at all because the bottom line was we were guided by the children. Our role was to guide the child to be successful.

With children taking the lead in showing their parents and educators what they wanted to photograph, their actions as much as their verbal communication were key clues:

> Children were given independence to take photographs. Particular children had particular needs and the teacher responded to those needs in terms of what the children wanted to photograph. A child would indicate what was wanted and take the teacher by the hand to show what he wanted to photograph.

Educators and parents alike scaffolded children's participation, encouraging and showing faith in their children:

> Educators worked with children's parents and gave parents the opportunity to be involved with their children in the process. Parents encouraged their children: 'You can do it. You can take four photographs.' Other parents said: 'You can have it for 10 minutes and when you've finished that, we'll go and do something else.' Some parents said: 'Let's go outside and we'll do some things outside.' Other parents said: 'Let's do what you are doing inside. Let's take some photographs of what you are doing inside.' Parents guided them and I allowed that to happen. If that's the way the parents chose to do it themselves and guide their children, I stepped back out of that. I allowed them to do whatever it was, and we sort of worked it out between the children, the parents and myself. So it was a three-way conversation all of the time about it.

Children's parents and educators remained with the children throughout these experiences. They observed what the children were doing, following behind and talking with children as they took photographs. As Nicola explained, the digital cameras presented as much of a learning curve for some of the adults as for some children:

> The teachers had to master the use of the camera and the children did it, too. They were co-learners. We were a community of learners, it was like a community of practice.

70 Photography in an Eyre and Western community

In this community of practice, educators, parents and children learned how to use the camera and what it would do – what its possibilities were for children exploring their local communities and expressing what is important to them. Watching children master the cameras in and of itself provided windows into children's capabilities:

> Just the learning of the camera and how to hold it, where to place it to get the photographs and what buttons to press, was a lot to learn. But the children got that down pat fairly quickly. Some had a little bit longer time to master that, but they all mastered that. After they got the idea of how to use the camera, they were up and going. They just took photograph after photograph, and in all sorts of places. The children were very open to it. They just took it in their stride. They worked out how the camera worked, and off they went.

Adults' discretionary judgment was critical in allowing time for children to enter into and negotiate these novel experiences. As described by Nicola, children explored: 'They'd hold the camera back to front or upside down.' Children showed deep curiosity: 'They wanted to see how it worked – what went in, where the batteries go. They asked lots and lots of questions like: "What does the button do?"' There were varied levels of expertise and experience among the children: 'Some children were savvier than others. Other children had no idea. So it sort of went from one extreme to the other.'

So what do these observations tell us so far about the dialogic encounter when consulting with young children, particularly children with preconceived limitations? That such encounter accommodates children's different levels of expertise and ways of knowing and doing. That in such encounter, adults trust the child more than any preconceived judgment about what the child can and cannot do. That the adult actively listens and watchfully engages as a co-learner with the child, and not separate from the child. That time is amply provided for children to explore and master the means by which the consultations are done:

> Once the children got the gist of the cameras, they went on all right. But some children did take a little longer to actually master how to actually use the camera because they kept on wanting to look *at* it instead of *through* it.

This observation brings us to another key message about the dialogic encounter when consulting with young children – that is, the process for children learning how to use consultations' tools of engagement is as dialogic as the consultations themselves. This process can be as revealing of what is important to children as anything they might say in direct answer to our questions. As Nicola herself concluded:

> It was just amazing. I just worked it through with the children, about, 'This is what we do to get it all to work', and all that sort of thing. But the children asked lots and lots of questions and they were busting to use the cameras.

Structures and modes that sustained dialogue

Some key structural changes made these consultations an effective and worthwhile experience for all involved? One such change was providing prolonged time for sustained engagement as children learned the tools of engagement and engaged in the dialogue that ensued. These new tools were incorporated into children's familiar repertoires of tools, particularly exploratory play.

Another key shift was removing constraints borne of preconceptions about *what* the children are (for example, developmentally delayed, disabled, impaired, poor) – and replacing these notions with an evolving understanding of *who* the children are. Educators worked collaboratively with parents, and all learned to stand back and see how children quickly learned through their own hands-on explorations how to use the cameras and take remarkable photographs of their everyday surrounds.

In coming to more deeply understanding who their children are, educators and parents shifted their interaction patterns and participant structures from 'doing *for* children' to 'doing *with* children' – a shift that required longer, more sustained engagement in the dialogic process of consultation. 'Doing with children' saw parents and educators step into children's playful ways that highlighted the vital part that play has in children exercising their citizenship – play and exploration, experimentation and practice, developing competence in using the modes through which they express their views:

> Children liked to look at the camera. They experimented with using the camera in different positions in relationship to themselves and their body. They'd push this or press that. 'Do I turn this?' They had the independence to do this on their own. They worked out the front or the back of the camera, or holding it upside down. Some of them wanted to use the camera upside down. Children put the camera in front of themselves, right in front of their face, that sort of thing. They were trying to work out how come it went around and why it made this sudden noise, or when you clicked it something went real bright. You know, that bright flash and that puzzled some of the children.

Igniting this exploration and dialogue was children's desire to engage – as Nicola observed: 'Children were very focused and engrossed with what they were doing. They *wanted* to do it.'

Children's themes

In relation to the central question framed in terms of what matters to children in this Eyre and Western community, four macro-categories of thematic interest emerged – people (self and others, including family, friends, neighbours, play-group and the staff in their home learning partnership programme, as important

72 Photography in an Eyre and Western community

people in their lives); home (rooms and indoor spaces; outdoor spaces and activities; toys and other belongings); pets, animals and nature; and places and activities further afield, including holidays and outings. We describe below how these themes manifested themselves in each child's photos and his or her accompanying talk, captions and non-verbal communication.

Georgia (age 3) took several self-portraits with the camera. She particularly tried to take photos of her own fingernails. While she managed to capture her fingers in part, photographing her fingernails eluded her. She snapped her family friend who babysat her and with whom she went on 'play dates to Hungry Jacks'; and included this photo in her 'favourite things' category, along with her bedroom with her bed, teddy bears and bedtime stories. They would read at least three stories each night before bedtime, with the bears in bed with her. Georgia took many photos of her trampoline, while both on and off it, especially after 'they had put sparkly crafty bits in it'. Photos show her looking through the trampoline's net and capture the sense of fast movement as she jumped up and down. Georgia also shot her brother's bike, explaining that at the top of the picture are 'some things' she uses in the dirt, 'like making cakes and digging there'. Georgia loved animals and took photos of her pet budgerigars, Tweety and Violet.

Michael (age 4) made a self-portrait by standing in front of a mirror and snapping his reflected image. The photo shows him from the waist up to the camera lens, the top of his head cut off and his face obscured from view. He was wearing a Bob the Builder T-shirt. His caption read: 'Bob the Builder. Michael photo.' According to Nicola, Michael was 'highly sensory, and was fascinated with the camera and he had great delight in taking lots of pictures. Each picture was very different. He worked out how to use it with limited assistance from his mother.' He took another photo of himself, with the camera held at waist level pointed up to his face – 'Michael take photo.' He captioned a photo he took of his foot while standing on a multi-coloured carpet, 'Green, red, blue. I like colours'. Another photo he took of his bare foot on a red carpet was captioned, 'The carpet feels nice'. Michael snapped his sister eating a cracker with peanut butter, which he described as 'Donna home from school'. Michael also photographed Nicola and labelled his photo, 'Nicola brings toys'. He took photos of two of his toys – 'My truck' and 'Shaun the sheep'. Michael enjoyed a range of different toys, books and puzzles. He photographed the home computer, with his caption, 'Take photo computer'. Michael also took a close-up shot of his pet cat's face in the sun, with the simple but emphatic, 'Alice!' Michael also enjoyed his small pup, wanting to hold and cuddle him often.

Quentin (age 4) had photos taken on his behalf by his mother during the consultations, cueing in to people, activities and objects that figured prominently and brought enjoyment in his life. These photos included members of his immediate and extended family. The caption to these snaps, with his mother's assistance, conveyed the message: 'I like to spend time with my family, doing special things together. I love sitting on my Grandma's lap, sitting next to my dad when we go on holidays in our motor home, and I like reading with my Uncle Geoff.' Quentin was learning to use a 'PODD communication book with lots of pictures in it that people use to tell me what we are about to do. I am also learning to use my big yellow switch that Mum calls a Step-by-Step to say "Hello" and "Goodbye" to people. Finally, I just love to make noises and smile at my favourite people.' Quentin's photos conveyed that he enjoyed 'doing lots of things, with Mum's help, when I'm at home. I enjoy popping with bubbles, pressing keys on the keyboard to make music, playing on the computer, and standing in my walker.'

William (age 4) took five photos of his toy planes with the captions: 'Big special plane 'cause I bought it at the shop . . . They are my fighter jets . . . It's a function jet . . . I was getting these [planes] out of the bag 'cause I wanted to take a photo of them. I love my planes.' William talked about his passion for planes, of which he has 'lots' as seen in his photos. He lined them up on his bedroom floor and also had planes hanging from his ceiling. He described the uses, colours and types of engines of his different planes and how he often flies them around his room. As he demonstrated flying the planes, he warned, 'You need to watch your head!' He enjoyed talking to everyone about his planes. William also took a photo of his legs and feet with the caption, 'These are my favourite shoes'. He photographed Nicola with the caption, 'That's Nicola'. He photographed his bike, with the caption, 'That's my Ben 10 bike. I go really fast!' He snapped 'the Kindy lizard' and 'Bonsai, my turtle. It looks like two bonsais' (Bonsai was in a mirrored tank).

Vincent (age 4) took lots of photos of mirrors and even more photos of his various toys. He was very excited about his photo of the toy bus and wanted to keep looking at it for a long time. He took several photos of the same toy plane in different locations in his home. He photographed his brother's toy and talked about it at length in terms of its eye that is all that is seen of the toy in the photo, and his own shoe-clad foot that lurk at the bottom of the photo's frame. In a similar vein, Vincent also snapped a toy on the living room floor, along with the floor mat, television and his own legs. The toy mat was itself the subject of many photos that captured different parts of the mat. Vincent also photographed his younger brother with his toys and playing with a toy phone. Vincent also took numerous photos of the ceiling and pedestal fans in his home showing very close-up details and various shots looking through his front screen door, including close-ups of the door's wire mesh. Television featured in some of Vincent's photos, with many a close-up shot of cartoon programmes.

Rachel (age 3) took a long-distance shot of a house with the back of a van to the left of the frame and a good deal of ground in the foreground. Her caption read, 'Blue van. Door. Dad lives here'. Rachel also snapped a close-up detail in this same setting showing a flowering plant in front of a water tank, with the front wheel of the blue van in the top right-hand corner. The caption, read, 'Yellow flowers and a wheel'. Rachel photographed her bedroom, a medium shot of her bed, with her caption, 'My bed. Pooh Bear, pillow'. Rachel enjoyed drawing,

74 Photography in an Eyre and Western community

especially drawing people's faces. She talked about their eyes, ears, noses, mouths and hair. She was learning to cut and loved to read. She brought a book to her educator and talked about the pictures as they read. In a photo Rachel arranged to have taken of herself, she was sitting on the living room floor amid an assortment of objects, with the caption, 'I am doing a bee puzzle'. Rachel photographed her pet animals, with captions she created: '"Moggy" – eyes, ears, tail, "meow" . . . Moggy and Norton and Eve – two dogs' . . . 'Three guinea pigs. They have a doggy bowl' . . . 'Horses and Honey – three horses' . . . '"Norton". He has ears, head, eyes, nose, mouth – pup' . . . 'Eve's tummy. You have got a tummy too. She has ears and she barks'. Out and about, Rachel photographed a vast expanse of empty beach. Her caption read, 'Beach – sand, water, sky, seaweed'.

Peter (age 3) had many photos of his family – his mum and dad, his sister with 'her tongue out', 'Nanna's feet', 'Grandad' who would spend lots of time with him, and cousins he named who also spent time together with him. Peter took photos of Adelaide, where he spent much time in hospital for treatment of his rare heart condition. When looking at these photos, he said his family 'had a holiday at the beach house', that he 'was not scared', and 'don't fall'. He described the merry-go-round where 'the music was noisy. It went slowly. We on there. Looking backwards.' He was excited about his photos taken from the hotel at breakfast time, asking: 'Is that the whole city?' A photo of a street scene was upside down, prompting Peter to say: 'The cars upside down. You're gonna fall from the sky.' He also took photos of the family car's interior. Peter had photos of his work with his physiotherapist and a visit to Kindergym, showing very close-up shots of parts of the gym's various pieces of equipment. He commented: 'I'm not in there. Run and jump. Yes, I do!' Peter also took photos of 'Peter's bits' – his hands in different positions, his feet together in the car, and his teeth when he had brushed them.

Patricia (age 3) took photos of her 'favourite things to do' – drawing, puzzles, dress-ups, and playing in her cubby house in the backyard. Her photos also showed Patricia and her family and friends enjoying a range of outdoor activities at home – riding a scooter, playing on adventure playground equipment, bathing in an inflatable swimming pool and going on a slide for the first time that she 'loved'. According to her mother, Patricia 'is in her element' when she is 'around animals . . . she is calm and confident. She just loves animals', as plainly evidenced in photos of Patricia with animals. Some of Patricia's photos showed her at an animal park, engaging closely with the animals, patting and stroking them. Her mother said that 'she did everything there'.

Robbie (age 3) had a photo of himself taken, sitting on his bedroom floor and playing with one of his toy cars. His caption read, 'Me car!' Robbie took several photos of his toy cars and trucks set out on the floor, camera pointed down on them from above, with his captions: 'Car and man and the "pump" . . . A blue car and orange balloon [with half an image of the balloon dominating the photo, and a number of cars on the corner of a floor car mat] . . . My cars – ice cream van, truck, bus and plane . . . My truck is yellow like the train.' Robbie had a pet guinea pig and rabbit and liked to hold them. He photographed the guinea pig, and composed its caption, '"Chumper". Chumper has a nose like me'. Robbie also took a photo of a snail – while this might have suggested he liked snails, the fact was he didn't. Apparently, he had what his educator called a 'pet passion' for squashing photos – this was the 'before' photo, with a caption that read, 'Baby more. Baby snails eyes'. Robbie photographed the wheel of his bike, 'A wheel same as train' and his bike helmet that he simply captioned, 'My helmet'. Robbie also photographed flowers in his garden and created the caption, 'Smell the flower'.

Owen (age 4) initiated making with his mother an album of the photos he took during the consultations. He included a collection of photos of himself, with the heading in very large font, 'ME'. His mother wrote: 'It did not take Owen long to work out how to turn the camera around to take photos of himself. He was most fascinated by how he looked. It didn't matter if it was his boot, his sock or his toes. He was particularly interested in the lines on his hands. He loves photos of Owen, they make him feel happy.' These photos showed head-and-shoulders photos of himself, a close-up photo of his eyes, another close-up of the open palm of one of his hands, another looking down at his bare feet, and another with his foot in a sock. He included photos of his neighbours who cared for his sister and he when their mother is at work, 'Grandad and Granny' and said, 'They're my best friends'. Owen also talked about his sister Haylee Jade and how he loved to play with her. His photos show his sister in their playroom at home, and photos of things that make his sister laugh. One photo was captioned: 'It's a jungle. Haylee Jade's cheeky monkey play music. Hayley laugh.' Another photo's caption read: 'I turn fans up the top on fast. The planes and cars move. Haylee laugh.' Owen also included photos of his father, who is a tradesman and whom Owen thought was like Bob the Builder. A photo of his father's van was captioned: 'Daddy got a flattie. I help him fix.' Owen also helped his father mend fences on their property. Photos of his father show him smiling and pulling a silly face because 'he loves to make Owen laugh'. Owen enjoyed his trains – in his own words, 'I love trains!' His photos depicted 'Grandad and Granny' with 'a bargain train set' that his mother bought at a garage sale, and close-up photos of the tracks and engines. Owen photographed the television and DVDs at home, with his caption, 'I need to watch cartoons!' Owen would recount favourite scenes from cartoons and movies, assisted by his merchandise toys. With a photo he took of such toys, he captioned: 'Lightning McQueen go real fast. Mack truck take him in the back. Check Brum out, he up the top.' Owen also said, 'I like to make things', a caption to a set of three photos. One photo showed felt pieces with Owen's caption: 'Nicola's toys are cool. Look, I made a rocket and rainbow.' Another photo showed his construction of a rocket, with the caption: 'Mummy helped me make this rocket. I put stars on it with glue.' The third photo showed children's paintings on a wall at home, with the caption: 'Haylee and me made these at playgroup. Mummy put them up with blu tac. I get blu tac and make a

76 Photography in an Eyre and Western community

ball.' Around his home, Owen liked to ride around the house with his sister, as his photos showed (the front yard, sister on a small tricycle, a close-up of white daisies in the garden, another close-up of his skateboard, Owen taking a photo of his shadow, and three photos of paddocks on their property. As an accompaniment to these photos, his mother wrote that Owen and his sister 'love exploring in the front yard, which they call "The Secret Garden". Owen often picks flowers from the garden for his mother and likes to play by the tank stand where an aquarium full of tiny, smooth, colourful rocks has been emptied. Owen likes the blue rocks. In fact, he likes any baby rocks. He sleeps with one often, always has one in his car seat, and Mum is forever finding rocks in the bottom of the washing machine.' Owen's caption on top of these three photos of farm paddocks read: 'The horses eat all the long grass. I help daddy and mummy build a bigger and bigger pile [of pruned and felled tree branches]. We make a hot bonfire and have marshmallows. Lots of birds go in the trees.' Owen photographed his bike and created the caption: 'My bike! I go faster and faster. I win!' Owen also took a close-up photo of his mother's bicycle, zooming in on the child's seat. The caption read: 'This is Mummy's bike. Haylee hop up the back and we go for ride. We go see [neighbours names]. I get the EGGS!' Owen's photos taken when getting the eggs include hens, ducks, eggs and a dog that he throws a ball to.

In their captions, comments and non-verbal communication, children revealed their attachment to what or whom the photos signified to them. Having a reason to talk was very empowering for children and led to meaningful conversation with their families and educators about what mattered to them – including children with significant language challenges:

> William can talk, but then again he'll only talk about certain things. So we managed to get him to talk about other things because he took photographs of some other things. So there were a few other photographs and things other than the cars.
>
> Robbie had a speech delay and his speech was limited. But the photos gave him something to focus on, and when children are focused on something, they don't think about the actual speech. It happens a bit more spontaneously.

So it was for the children who engaged in these consultations in this Eyre and Western community that the photos gave them an authentic and profoundly felt reason to talk and prompted their language use – as Nicola put it, 'they wanted to do it'.

Reflecting on the Eyre and Western case study

Earlier in this chapter, we described how, during this encounter, a child would take his teacher by the hand to show what he wanted to photograph. This image

Photography in an Eyre and Western community 77

provides an evocative metaphor for co-construction, empowering children's participation and releasing their agency in this dialogic space.

At the outset of these consultations, the programme's director was concerned about how children and families would 'cope', in view of their perceived learning and developmental issues and their low SES or downright impoverished circumstances that saw many not in possession of or familiar with cameras.

What initially was seen to be a potential problem or limitation, however, transformed into opportunity and provocation for children to develop expertise with digital photography and for children and their families alike to be able to visually document their experiences and themselves. Deepening relationships with children that came from viewing children's worlds through their eyes, saw educators and families move beyond the limitations they perceived their children had. They came to know their children, and children came to know themselves, a good deal more than they did before the consultations began. In short, the consultations as dialogic encounter constituted an empowering experience for all concerned:

> It was incredible just watching the children. Their enthusiasm! They enjoyed what they were doing. The children were just in awe of the cameras and what they could do with them. The very fact that the children were taking photographs was, gosh, it was just amazing. There was no stopping them! All of us, parents and myself, we were just amazed with what the children did with them. It was incredible just watching them.

These dialogic consultations not only allowed adults to see the children's world in a new light – children came to see themselves in a new light. Their cries of delight, such as 'Look what I've done!' and 'Look what I've got!' were frequently heard as children took and viewed their photographs. Children were seen to be proud of their achievements and bolstered by the success that was theirs.

Photos saw children explore their own identity and how they sense themselves in their world. One child snapped his own shadow, but when his educator showed him the print, he became quite upset as he could not see his face in the shadow and thought he had lost his face. Rushing to a mirror inside, the educator was able to reassure the child that his face was still there, and talk more about shadows and what they represented.

When a child with autism photographed himself and then looked at his picture, his educator noted:

> It was like he had discovered himself. He couldn't quite believe that there he is *here*, but he's also out *there* in the photograph. We couldn't talk it through because he didn't have that understanding, but he could recognise himself, which was amazing . . . He was very proud of what he did and he took quite a few photographs of himself. He kept looking at the photograph of himself

78 Photography in an Eyre and Western community

on the camera. Every now and then he would touch himself as if to say, 'That's me'. That was amazing, just watching him look and gaze at his own photograph. His mum and I got quite teary about it. It was really quite an emotional time. His mum said: 'He's just realised who he is.' I said: 'Yes, that's what's happened. He's taken a photograph of himself and he's realised that it's him he's looking at.'

This awakening of the child's conscious awareness of himself and his presence in the world – a particularly dramatic and poignant example of what Freire (1983) calls conscientisation – had an impact on his family:

I went back there a few times to see how Mum was going and said: 'If it gets a bit too overwhelming, then it's OK to stop.' I wasn't quite sure. He went on to take some other photographs, and some lovely photographs too. But he did like the photograph of himself and he just kept going back to it. When his mum put it up on the computer, well, he was so excited. When his sister and dad got home, he wanted to show them. And he came and he touched the computer, and he was touching the photo, and so they put it up for him and he was showing them – proud of what he did and wanting to share it with the family. And they responded.

Impact was found to extend to children's fathers, who did not engage directly with their children in these consultations. As Nicola's observations revealed:

Children's conversations opened up with their families. The dads came in. I mean none of the dads were home at the time [in the day when children took their photos]. But when they got home, they came on board with the children . . . The fathers were thrilled to bits and they've gone on with their children with the camera work, and they've included the other children in the family, and that sort of thing. Because all of them have other family members, it's become an evolving thing. It's brought some of the families that were a little bit disjointed, it's brought them together because they've got this camera. It's amazing.

Nicola's observation was further supported and illustrated with this example:

There's one family, they're a little bit disjointed at times, and, you know, they're a family that's really struggling in life. This experience has brought them together because they've gone out to take photographs as a family, to take photographs of what they are doing as a family. Well, that hadn't been happening before at all.

Such observations were evidenced in other families too, where parents were separated and in families who currently didn't have cameras or never had owned

Photography in an Eyre and Western community   79

a camera before, and so their children had never seen a camera (as we noted earlier in this chapter). For example:

> It's brought them together as families, particularly like William and his mum and his dad, I think Dad only has him for short periods of time but they had another conversation to talk about, instead of arguing about lots of things. It's brought another family together, too, because now they've got this camera, they're using it a lot. Whenever they go out now, they take the camera and they're all taking photographs. They are a very low socio-economic family. Dad hasn't got work, so it's given them more reason to go out. Now they have the camera, they go down to the beach more often with the family . . . Mums and dads who are separated have got something more in common to talk about, and parents have pictures of the children in both homes.

Children's siblings also became involved:

> Rachel's family . . . they'd never, never had a camera, so that was really good and beneficial to them as a family, brought them together as a family. Rachel has an older disabled brother and that's been very powerful in their family because he himself enjoyed doing photographs with and for Rachel and children taking turns to use the camera.

One family rang to tell Nicola they had 'taken a hundred photographs' – the family was 'thrilled' and the fact they initiated this call reflected the empowerment they felt that comes from seeing and validating the competent child – *their* competent child.

Observing the impact of this whole dialogic experience, and not the cameras alone (which families were able to keep after the consultations had finished), Nicola found herself reflecting more:

> I was absolutely astounded with what came out with the families . . . It has been very powerful. It's had a big effect on families. It was just an extension of my work. It took a bit of extra time in my normal running. But it's been really, really worthwhile and it's been lovely to see the families blossom. It was a real privilege to work with these children very specifically and to watch the children blossom and grow, and families blossom, and to watch the parents delight in what was happening . . . and to see the parents enjoy it with their children. So thank you for allowing me to be a part of it. It was lovely to watch the children delight in it and their parents delight in their children's activities, and that was very special.

Just as educators and families felt empowered by this experience, so too did the children. As Nicola put it 'every child had something that was really important to

80 Photography in an Eyre and Western community

them' that they expressed. Encapsulated in this simple but quite powerful observation are ideals of faith, humility and trust that infused this Eyre and Western encounter. As Freire (1983, p. 79) has written, dialogue requires 'intense faith' in people, as well as humility: 'How can I dialogue if I always project my ignorance onto others and never perceive my own?'

Freire's vision of dialogue was framed by mutual trust among participants that grows from faith and humility. In this Eyre and Western community's consultations, trust grew in terms of adults trusting in the children's competence and insights, and children trusting in adults that the encounter would be worthwhile, it would be true to them, and that its outcomes would be heeded.

Founded on such trust, this encounter was a space where children expressed their views and showed their world to others through their own lens, while also showing and seeing themselves anew through that same lens. The children took delight in equal measure in both these accomplishments – evidenced in their remarks like, 'Oh, that's my dog!', 'Oh, look what I did!', 'That's my photo!' and 'That's me!'

Chapter 6

Children weave their desires into a shared vision for their Fleurieu community

I wish I had a huge adventure playground. My friend Milly and I would play there together. The butterflies there would play with us, flying all around the bright flowers. I feel happy at the adventure playgrounds.

(Joanne, age 7)

At an out-of-school-hours care (OSHC) service, children were engaged in the consultations through creating textile images on calico squares that were sewn together as a patchwork quilt-like wall hanging. Children's expression of material themes was infused with their social themes that related to their sense of solidarity and wellbeing from being connected with others. These social themes remained constant even as children's expression of their material desires shifted from day to day in this encounter. The quilt-like wall hanging gave scope for both individual expression and a synthesis that found common ground and brought together children and their ideas – thus underscoring the core message from these children that the whole (their social whole) is more than the sum of its parts (their material wishes and interests).

Contextual information

This case study's OSHC service for children five to twelve years was located in the Fleurieu and Kangaroo Island region that experienced below average unemployment levels, with mainly managerial, associate professional, trades and labourer occupations.

This Fleurieu service operated at three local primary schools and serviced the families and children from two local co-educational colleges. The programme valued children's social development, as well as time and opportunity for children to interact with their friends. Activities in the programme fostered children's development of life skills and problem-solving capabilities, and nurtured children's own talents and interests. The programme, framed by Australia's national framework for OSHC, *My time, our place* (DEEWR, 2011) was designed to complement children's learning in their home and school settings through leisure

82 Shared vision for a Fleurieu community

and play. It was in the spirit of leisure and play, therefore, that the educators approached the consultations with their children.

Framing purpose and problem for engagement

Working collaboratively with one another and the area's early childhood consultant (a regionally-based DECS employee with curriculum expertise), this Fleurieu OSHC service's educators developed and documented a strategic plan for the consultations. This plan envisaged the consultations as a staged process and emphasised the importance of developing shared understanding with children about the purpose of the consultations, and how in general but flexible terms the consultations would unfold. One educator 'took hold of the project' in terms of coordination and maintaining consistency in their approach across the three sites. The plan took stock of:

- Informing and explaining the consultations and their intent to all staff in the service and Governing Council (the governing body of a service with a majority parent membership).
- Informing and explaining the consultations and their intent to all parents, caregivers and children.
- Informing all other participating parties and organising dates for their participation.
- Determining what resources would be needed and how to most effectively use the $1,000 budget provided by DECS to the site (as all sites) for the consultations.
- Discussing how children would be consulted, and considering questions that would be meaningful for children and make their thoughts visible.
- Discussing how children's ideas would be documented.
- Determining the time frame for the consultations.
- Discussing how to collect and collate individual children's ideas into one presentation and planning a launch event to celebrate children's views.

In initial brainstorming sessions, educators decided upon their core strategy – children would use textile art pens to draw what they wished for in their communities on individual A4-sized pieces of calico that would be sewn together as a wall hanging resembling a quilt. This activity would involve discussion and drafting of ideas, and mediation of ongoing dialogue with and among children about their community views and desires.

The wall hanging idea was borne of much discussion of alternative ideas, including film-making or creating a children's current affairs programme. However, the educators believed it was important to keep the process relatively simple so as to maximise opportunity and time for reflective dialogue in the context of what is a time-challenged OSHC space. The individual pieces meant that children could create these works at different times, given variations across children's attendance patterns that typify OSHC services, and so increase inclusion of all children who wished to participate. Staff also wished their approach to be conducive to recognising and respecting individual children's input, while also being able to work towards a product that would contain a synthesis of the children's ideas. The wall hanging was able to meet all these requirements.

In their vision of the consultation process, educators explicitly emphasised 'fun tools . . . bright colours and thought-provoking questions' that they hoped would set this project apart from children's regular classroom work during school hours – bearing in mind that these children would be engaging in the consultations outside their school hours. Educators were adamant that this dialogic consultation would 'not be about sitting in a classroom and producing a piece of work', mindful that even creating a work of art might be seen by some children to be mandatory, assessable work, which would go against the grain of the consultations.

In keeping with this spirit, staff designed posters to make the purpose and process of the consultations accessible for children, families and staff alike. The director explained that staff deigned the posters to be 'bright, fun and easy to read, inviting children to participate . . . We put the posters up around the centre and handed the invites to the children.' The poster's headline read: 'What do you wish for?' Beneath this headline was a call to action – 'Calling all children. We want to hear your ideas of how we can make SA a better place to live.' An enticement was added in multi-coloured font – 'Would you like to draw, paint and create?' An explicit invitation was set out at the bottom of the poster: 'You are invited to participate in an activity involving artistic expression. What is important to you? Let's get creative. We will use art in a fun way to voice our ideas, thoughts and feelings.'

While children were given time to digest the posters and think and talk about their participation, staff calculated costs of canvas sheets and textile pens for the wall hanging and created a simple A4-sized template for children's drawings. The template had a simple framing border, headed with the central question of the consultation, 'What is important to children and what do children wish for in their lives?' and a space for the child's name and age at the bottom of the page. Educators also observed that the templates they developed for children's individual drawings (previously described) helped develop 'a sense of belonging' among the children in terms of 'ownership, with the child's name at the top and a heading for them'.

Staff next handed out personal invitations to children, which were miniature versions of the posters. These invitations were accompanied by letters to children's parents and caregivers requesting permission for their children to participate. As Annette, the director, explained:

> We had conversations with the children about the process and what we had planned . . . Children needed to understand what they were working

towards, the question at the heart of the consultations, 'What did they want for their future?' It was important that staff showed evidence that it was a collaborative working with children and listening to their needs. We wanted children to understand what the staff were doing and to be a part of the process.

Educators collaboratively developed six key questions to pose and explore in dialogue with children, all centring on what was important to children in their community and what they wished for in their lives. The questions were:

- Where do you go in your community?
- What activities do you enjoy?
- Who do you like to spend time with?
- What do you like at your favourite place?
- How do you feel about your community?

So it was that children began to engage with educators on a one-to-one basis in small group settings to dialogue, draft and sketch their ideas about their community views and desires.

How the encounter unfolded

Dialogue germane to these consultations was sparked by creative tools, a call to action, and a collaborative approach that gave scope for individual expression and blue-sky thinking. The posters, invitations and ensuing dialogue began the development of shared understandings about the purpose of the consultations, the way in which these consultative conversations and activities were to occur, and concepts about the future.

Educators reported that the children were 'excited' to be engaged this way. Educators also observed the effect of small groups on others in the centre who did not engage at first – interest in the project activity quickly extended to these other children. Children intently engaged in small group settings, indoors and outdoors, at a table or on the floor or grass, alone or with others, as evidenced in the photos taken throughout this encounter. Clearly, the children enjoyed the creativity and novelty afforded by the artistic materials at hand. Just as apparent was children's appreciation that their voices were being authentically listened to.

Over time, the children drafted, sketched and talked about their initial ideas. While dialogue scaffolded children's process of articulating and developing their ideas, there was no scaffolding for how children artistically drafted their ideas – in this area of the consultations, children were left to call on their own devices and talents. Educators saw the children's ultimate artistry residing in how children explained their ideas and drawings to others – so it was that educators focused their scaffolding efforts on children's verbal reflections. This scaffolding used open-ended questions and prompts to ensure children's ideas were respected.

Not that there were not any challenges. Indeed, educators observed a number of issues in these dialogic consultations. One such issue was that some children wanted to copy ideas from others in their small groups. Educators found this process worked best when children were able to work separately from their peers and develop their own individual responses.

Another challenge concerned tension between children's present and future thinking – as an educator described the situation, 'children were not thinking past the "now" ... We were getting the children's ideas through drawing about what they want now, not necessarily the future.' This tension was resolved through careful dialogue about concepts of the present and the future. Educators found that while the drawing initially anchored children's thinking in the present, ensuing dialogue was able to extend children's reflections into the future.

Another challenge related to children's fleeting wishes that changed from day to day throughout this process:

> Children wanted something different each day. Children want something different because it's the new trend or it's cool – it's about peer influence.

These issues are important for how we think about engaging with children's voices. It is not enough to talk with children about what they want. We need to engage deeply in ongoing dialogue and clarify its terms of engagement. We need to explore more and more deeply what underlies children's wants – their thematic concerns and what makes life valuable and worthwhile to them. We need, too, to carefully observe children and understand from how they act in their world what is important to them.

When children were satisfied with their drafts, they rendered their final drawings onto calico squares that were then sewn together to make the wall hanging with the label, 'What do you wish for?'

Structures and modes that sustained dialogue

The wall hanging was a visually powerful way of conveying children's individual and collective views – it also ensured that children, families and other interested parties could see what children expressed was important to them in their communities.

As Freire (1983) maintained, if our existing structures do not allow and sustain dialogue, then we need to change those structures. There were a number of structural issues with which educators contended during this encounter. One such issue related to resources. There was no colour printer in the centre to create the colourful posters, invitations and other related materials that staff wished to provide children and families to impart a sense of enjoyment and pleasure in the experience. So staff used a home computer instead. The staff camera unfortunately broke down, making it difficult to retrieve photos from the camera. Binding for the final report was initially a problem but educators were assisted by the regional DECS office of their early childhood consultant.

Time also was seen to be a constraint on educators' capacity for gathering children's many ideas for how the consultations might be done, which were explored in the planning stage. Educators were concerned that not all children were included in the project and, in their own words, would have liked to have been able to be inclusive so 'it was equitable . . . It's important for the children to be listened to and we were concerned that this wasn't weighted in the process because of the time factor.'

Children's attendance patterns were an added consideration. Some children spent less time than others in this encounter because of attendance – some children attended the service every weekday, while other children did not attend every day. Consequently, accessing children to continue working on their piece or clarify and elaborate on its meaning was sometimes difficult.

Therefore, as an educator explained, 'having a key message coming from each child and incorporating it into a group package to get a presentation together was really hard'.

Educators resolved these constraints by creating an experience that was achievable with the time and resources they had at their disposal, and which allowed for children's individual input and collation as a group statement – as we have described in this chapter. In their approach, contending with structural constraints emerges as a matter of deciding what structures we can change and how and what in ourselves and our practices we can change to work with structures that, for the time being at least, seem somewhat immutable. The patchwork quilt-like wall hanging of children's messages that resulted proved ultimately effective, as evidenced in the documentation of children's themes that emerged.

Children's themes

Children expressed myriad views about their communities and what they wished for in their future lives. Children identified material needs in their community that focused on places and amenities. Some of these suggestions were geared to moderate activity, others were more action-packed. Some ideas were anchored in reality, while others were more futuristic or fantasy-oriented:

> I wish we had a music shop, ten-pin bowling alleys and an in-ground swimming pool. I would like my community to have these places because we don't have any of these things. We would really love these places and use them a lot.
>
> (Vince, age 12)

> I would like to have a skate park near my house where I can do all sorts of jumps and tricks. I feel really good when I ride my skateboard.
>
> (Paul, age 6)

I wish for a skate park and the longest toy train set which we could all ride on. I would be really happy to drive it every day.

(Martin, age 5)

I wish for a motor bike track. There are no bike tracks near my house and I feel happy when I'm on my bike. I like to do lots of tricks. My cousin drives his bike on big tracks. I love to watch him.

(Steven, age 5)

I would really wish for a BMX track in my area. It would have three massive jumps and have one smaller one.

(Nicholas, age 7)

I wish for a park full of diggers and tractors. We could dig huge sand castles.

(Henry, age 5)

I like fast things, especially the red bull cars that race really fast. I would like to wish for a skate and bike park near an in-ground swimming pool. I would be very happy if it was near my house. It could even have a roof over it all.

(Mark, age 8)

I wish for a play land, because it would be fun for kids instead of school lessons. We could learn tricks and other things there. I would feel happy because I would be having fun.

(Terry, age 6)

I wish I was the owner of Sea World. It would be really good to have a Sea World near my house. I would fix the animals and make a lot of money for the Sea World.

(Zac, age 7)

I wish for a technology centre where there are lots of tools to build transformers, machines and inventions. We could all go there to make our own inventions and stuff. I really like to make my own things with tools.

(Ian, age 6)

I wish for a very magical garden full of flowers and fairies.

(Vanessa, age 5)

I wish for a huge Lego World full of castles with big rocks around it and a moat. I feel happy when I'm creating my Lego castles. I have lots at home myself.

(Levi, age 6)

88 Shared vision for a Fleurieu community

> I wish for a big huge cupcake-shaped playhouse. We can make all sorts of fun things there.
>
> (Nicky, age 8)

> I would love a party garden with balloons and ribbons in it all the time. I feel excited and happy with lots of flowers and pretty party parks around.
>
> (Lisa, age 6)

These comments represent quite a wish list of places and things to do. It would be revealing to understand and talk with children more deeply about why these places and activities are important to them. We can infer reasons in some of their comments, but what is it, for example, that makes a child feel really happy when he is riding high on his skateboard, and how does he feel in other circumstances? These children's sense of positive wellbeing emerged in many of their comments – for example:

> Music is fun and makes me happy. I would like to be a hip-hop dance teacher making up my own dance routines. My special place I feel happy is my bedroom where I can sing and dance. My wish would be a dance school for teenagers which is free and this could be everyone's favourite place.
>
> (Hannah, age 12)

Hannah's comment about the school being free highlights another thematic concern that emerged among these children – accessibility and affordability of places and activities they would like to experience. For example:

> I would love to see a library in my town. I live there with all my family and we don't have one nearby. I love to read and would like to be able to walk there.
>
> (Vicky, age 9)

Inherent in Erin's comment is a desire to be independent, to walk instead of bus or drive, and to be able to pursue her reading interests. Other children expressed desires for nurturing their interests and learning in ways that would be accessible and affordable for their families, for example:

> I wish for a piano school in my local community. The community could do all free music and singing lessons. We could all do singing and perform for one another. Playing the piano makes me feel really happy.
>
> (Geneva, age 9)

> I wish for a dance school in my town. I love to dance. It keeps me busy. I like being energetic and move around a lot. It makes me feel great. We need

more dance schools that are free for everybody to join in. Dancing lessons shouldn't be about the money.

(Olivia, age 10)

I wish for a singing school of music. I love to sing. It makes me feel happy and excited. Everyone in the community could come there and we could join together and make performances to show.

(Victoria, age 9)

These comments reflect a community-mindedness coupled with personal interests collectively enjoyed. Clearly the question of fees and affordability posed issues for some children, providing grist for further dialogue with children about how such issues might be resolved.

Several children's comments about the places they would like to have in their communities revealed the importance of social amenity and sense of community that certain places afford:

I love to cook for other people. I wish there was a cooking school where children can learn to cook and make yummy things for their mums and dads. We need a kids' kitchen where all the benches, ovens and sinks were at our height.

(Rosie, age 7)

I wish for a gymnastics stadium as we only have one room here and you cannot do much in there. We need more equipment too! When I'm doing gym with friends, I feel really happy. I have lots of places I wish were closer to my house, like adventure parks where in the holidays I would hang out with my friends. My friends are very important to me.

(Rebecca, age 10)

I wish for a bowling alley for my local community where I could go with my family. I like to bowl with Billy. He makes me laugh.

(Anthony, age 7)

I wish for a big, big swing in a playground where lots of my friends can go on at the same time. It would be really fun for everyone.

(Louise, age 5)

I wish we could have a big adventure playground that has everything the whole family can play on together. I like having lots of friends to play with, too. So we can all meet up and have family barbecues and parties.

(Francine, age 7)

90   Shared vision for a Fleurieu community

> I wish I had a swimming pool. I love swimming with my family. I can swim now.
>
> (Bobby, age 5)

> I wish for a mini-golf course to be built in my area. I really enjoy hitting the golf ball with my dad and I would love it to be built real soon.
>
> (Tony, age 8)

> I wish for a mini-golf course in my area where I could meet up with my friends and we can play games.
>
> (Winston, age 10)

> I wish I had a huge adventure playground. My friend Milly and I would play there together. The butterflies there would play with us, flying all around the bright flowers. I feel happy at the adventure playgrounds.
>
> (Joanne, age 7)

Revealing as these comments are about the entwining of children's physical worlds with their social worlds, well might we interrogate what comments such as these reveal about children's broader thematic concerns related to being with others and their vision for their world. Such dialogue, too, could explore how in practical, realistic terms, children might begin to realise their vision in the here-and-now, over and beyond imparting their views to their state government authority. How, for example, might children in co-operation with the government and others in their community be part of the solution to the problems they pose?

Sometimes, the entwining of children's social worlds with their material ones was not always harmonious for the children. Being with others could be problematic, and in some instances children sought quarantine from certain other parties. For example:

> I wish for a kids-only cake shop where we can go and cook our own cakes. We can do them for parties and sell them to our friends and teachers.
>
> (Mikala, age 9)

> I would love to have a big rainbow garden where nobody can get sick. Also at school, I would like a girls-only school with a student lunch room where we can hang out for lunch.
>
> (Olivia, age 8)

> I wish for a skate park near my house where little kids can go to and not get pushed off by the big kids. I can do a few tricks and feel happy when I'm on my bike and skateboard.
>
> (Bobby, age 6)

Shared vision for a Fleurieu community 91

I wish that there was no bullying and littering in Australia. I feel depressed when I see bullying. I'd like everyone to get along in a nice clean environment, too. Sometimes when you feel like you're stranded on an island, you just have to, well, ignore it and be done with it. I just try and think about fun stuff.

(Sharon, age 9)

These comments are indicative of these children's significant concerns and form the basis of ongoing, collaborative problem-solving dialogue: Why are there bullies? How do children learn to be bullies? How might we deal with bullies and solve the bullying problem? What can adults do? What can children do?

Some children wished they could continue to 'play and have fun' at their Fleurieu OSHC house once they go to high school, when they stop being eligible for attending an OSHC service. An educator commented:

After the age of attending this OSHC service, there's nothing for them to do. They go to high school and stop being kids. The OSHC house is a place they can come and play, enjoy and feel safe and supported. Children are left at home once they turn thirteen.

Looking after animals emerged as a thematic interest for some children:

I wish to have my own vet company where I could treat all the local animals for free. I feel happy around animals and love to fix them when they cannot get help from anywhere.

(Harry, age 10)

I wish there was a turtle rescue facility in my town where we could save all the turtles that get hurt, lost or damaged. I am happy to work there and feel really good about helping the environment.

(Louise, age 10)

I wish there was a big dog park where we could take our pet dogs to go for a run with other dogs and they can make friends. I would like a safety fence around it so that the dogs are all safe. That would encourage exercise for everyone in the community.

(Rosemary, age 12)

Benefits for others in the community emerged in many of the children's previous comments, too. Most explicitly and perhaps most potently in its simplicity, is this child's vision:

I wish that everyone has a place to live.

(Lara, age 10)

92 Shared vision for a Fleurieu community

While including individual wishes in the final report, educators and children co-constructed a synthesis of what the children said they would like for their future, reflected in the wall hanging made up of their individual drawings sewn together. The synthesis went like this:

> The children of this Fleurieu OSHC service would like a happy, healthy eco-friendly environment where the animals are cared for free and the playgrounds are bustling with bright flowers, butterflies and adventure playgrounds. Music and dance are important to the children and they find the lessons expensive and hard to access. Skate parks and dirt bike tracks are a great way to keep active and create fun and happiness. The children expressed their love of cakes and cooking for others and made it clear they would like a child-friendly facility in which they could learn culinary skills.

Reflecting on the Fleurieu case study

Children's manifest enthusiasm in these consultations came from being actively involved in the project and being given the opportunity to talk and express their wishes and their underlying desires for their lives and the community where they lived.

This dialogic encounter, fruitful in its processes, provocative in its simple questions, and revealing in children's comments, provided a basis for ongoing dialogue that goes beyond the scope of the consultations but worthy of our consideration here in Freirean terms. We previously signalled such possibilities as we presented and discussed children's comments.

In this dialogic encounter, we see children's growing consciousness of their place in the world in relation to others. Therein lie implications for moving to more explicit problem-solving dialogue with these children. Wishes are not realised simply by telling someone what one wishes for – even if that someone is a state government authority who has solicited children's views.

To more fully realise the vision of citizenship presented in Chapter 1, it is both important and necessary to consider the deeper desires these children's wishes signify, and how collectively children might work together to make some of their shared vision a reality – thereby continuing to exercise their rights and responsibilities as citizens of the world in dialogue with others.

Some might say such action would assist these children to continue to develop as people or as citizens – we would say, these children are people and citizens already. We need to continue the dialogue with these children, deepening reflection to inform action – action of others, action of the government and action of themselves.

Chapter 7

Children express their views through music, drama and play in a Western Adelaide community

A magic space where things can happen.

(Theatre performer)

In this case study, we see children projecting themselves into a changed world that was their regular 'kindy' space. In this projection, we see children re-imagining themselves and their surrounds and exploring possibilities for what their communities could be. To the responsive observer and watchful listener, children revealed much about what was important to them – as much through the process of their dialogic, playful explorations as through the outcomes of what children actually said mattered to them.

Contextual information

This Western Adelaide children's service was situated in a suburban locality in a capital city's metropolitan area. The service's region experienced below average income levels and fluctuating unemployment levels. Occupations were chiefly professional, semi-professional and clerical in nature.

The children's service was a purpose-built children's centre for early childhood learning, development and parenting, and part of a birth-Year 12 (post-compulsory schooling) college. The service included long-day care children from six weeks of age, and sessional preschool. Also involved in the consultations at this site were children and staff of the college's out-of-school-hours care service. Community membership and partnerships among educators, families and communities were valued in the design and delivery of the centre's programmes, so as to nurture children's sense of belonging in their family and community contexts. The centre's programme focused on children's literacy and numeracy in challenging learning experiences, and valued and fostered children's creativity. The centre had access to a wide range of language, arts and computer experiences available in its college setting.

Framing purpose and problem for engagement

With a focus on using music, drama and play in their dialogic consultations with children about their local communities, staff and children worked with an early childhood adviser and a local theatre group. A musician, a choreographer, a theatre maker and a designer were involved, with the theatre group's director overseeing the work in collaboration with educators. Tracey, a DECS Head Office early childhood adviser, observed and interpreted what was happening and supported ongoing decisions about how the consultations might unfold. Together, this group co-operatively planned the consultations and reflected at the end of each day on how the consultations were proceeding and what to do the following day. This process empowered children to express themselves through artistic means to inform their government on policies for 'child friendly' communities.

Accordingly, a provocation was set up in one of the centre's rooms, to engage children with thinking about their local communities and what they wished for in their lives. This provocation initially took the form of a large ground sheet transformed through the power of imagination into a 'magic carpet'. The five-metre floor cloth provided a magical space in which 'anything was possible'. The use of the floor cloth was re-imagined into many possibilities by adapting the use of boxes and providing a wall to the magic carpet through a blank canvas of cardboard that children were able to paint on throughout the process. The emphasis throughout was to ensure children determined how the space and materials were used and shaped according to their thoughts and feelings that evolved over time as did the use of the materials.

As the first day progressed, large empty cardboard boxes, pillows and mats were placed on the floor for children and adults to engage in dramatic play. As children came into the room, they saw the performers in different positions in this space – a musician sat next to the piano, a performer lay down on the pillows on the ground, another performer positioned himself by the empty boxes, while another performer stretched out on the mats on the ground.

The performers engaged with the children who chose to step in this space and through their dramatic play, explored its possibilities in terms of their own local communities. Children used the boxes in various ways to explore and express themselves, and worked with these same materials in different ways to discover and express new layers of meaning.

A key challenge that arose when planning the consultations and this initial provocation related to preconceptions about children. The performers had not worked previously with young children, and felt a little uncertain about how to best approach this engagement. However, what initially was felt to be a challenge proved to be a strength contributing to the success of the consultations at this site, as Tracey observed. Precisely because the performers did not have preconceptions about particular children and how they might engage, they took their cues from the children – and so the consultation process became all the more dialogic, with children taking the lead in expressing their views, supported and inspired by the materials and structures that were provided and the adults with whom they co-constructed the experience.

How the encounter unfolded

As children initially approached the transformed space of ground sheets and mats, pillows and boxes, they were quite hesitant – as Tracey observed:

> They weren't quite sure how to take it – an adult lying on the ground! . . . One little guy just walked in, and because it was all so different, he just went 'Party, party party!' This is not normal Kindy!

Another child approached an adult lying on the floor who, according to Tracey observing this interaction,

> was very concerned that she might have been sick. Then there was a child who sat nearby on a chair who we found out later on, did have some issues around communication and being able to engage. He sat and watched for a long time, but it was her that he chose to go to, because she was on the ground, really physical with her pillows. And he suddenly felt this invitation to be able to engage with her and it didn't involve any talking or anything. So that was something that really stood out for me.

Another child approached the same adult lying on the ground and whispered: 'You're an *adult*!' Clearly this adult was not conforming to the child's expectations of adult behaviour from a child's point of view. In the face of such persistent behaviour by the performers, it was the children who reframed *their* preconceptions. This re-framing resonates with Freire's notion (1983) that as humans, we are all in the process of becoming . . . that is, becoming more fully human, more fully formed. In this sense, what it means to be an adult is similar to what it means to be a child, changing and growing. These children's space they called 'kindy' was also transforming, shifting from constraints of how things are or should be, to how things might be.

As the four days of this encounter progressed, it became more focused on children exploring and expressing their ideas and feelings about their communities. Educators and children worked with the same materials in different ways, to make it more engaging and explore deeper layers of meaning.

As the children engaged they became increasingly excited and wanted to come every day to take part. This enthusiasm and deep engagement was especially noteworthy for those children who were perceived to have communication and behaviour issues. These issues rarely surfaced in this engagement – performers took their lead from all the children, reading both their verbal and non-verbal cues, which authenticated and deepened children's involvement. For example, some children commented that the boxes needed more doors to change the configuration of the space and provided a way for the children inside the boxes (a possibly scary place with no light) to see the outside and feel safe – thus balancing a sense of adventure and risk taking with knowing it is undertaken in a controlled environment that is safe. One of the performers explained this taking of cues from children:

> The really interesting moments happen when children make a suggestion about something and not jump into the first instance of saying, 'No, that's not right because it doesn't fit my preconceived ideas', but to actually listen to what the child is saying, and saying, 'Is this a proposition that's worth taking forward and to developing it a bit further?' That wasn't chaotic. It was actually just taking time to listen to the child, and I found that really fascinating.

As the process continued to unfold, the performers showed what Tracey described as 'a complete interest in the children' and 'trusted in the children and the process'. Children and adults alike played with the same materials in different ways, in the spirit of co-construction with one another:

> One performer was inside one of the boxes and children could see a finger coming out of the box. Another day, they made doors into the boxes so children could create a house and get inside. Performers had an idea of why they were using the boxes and what was the purpose. They used the boxes as a plan but were totally responsive to where the children were going with it.

Performers were responsive to what children wished and needed, and could interpret and support children's clarification and elaboration about their themes, assisting in assembling and disassembling props that reflected and generated children's ideas.

Educators and performers found working with small groups of children worked better than working with a large group, which proved in their own words to be 'quite chaotic'. Adults worked with children in groups of five. Each group had their own space that allowed adults to 'hear the children's voices' in terms of reducing ambient noise and enhancing active listening to each child. As one educator put it, 'Smaller groups means you can hear the children's voice, not necessarily the loudest. We could respond to the individual rather than going with the loudest voice at the time' – or indeed, tuning into what children were showing and expressing through their non-verbal means.

As children engaged in dramatic play in these spaces, they transformed their realities – such is the power of play in children's lives, and such is the value of play in engaging children in dialogic consultations about their worlds. Children dressed up and 'got into character', and imagination rendered their carpet a 'magic carpet' that took them to different places and new ideas and ways of thinking about their worlds. There was no limit on how to use their space or how to transform it.

The dancer and choreographer in the theatre group made similar observations, noting that children without hesitation took up all challenges to exercise any choice they were given and expressed joy in doing so. This did not mean that children did not enjoy repeating activities but they preferred to engage in a number of different stimuli and possibilities before repeating activities.

Structures and modes that sustained dialogue

Much has already been said in this chapter of the use of play to transform space, empower thinking and sustain dialogue in these consultations at this Western Adelaide centre. In this space, children functioned in their own particular, preferred ways. Some children wanted to actively be involved in the thick of the activities, others were captured in the moment by the wonder of the possibilities unfolding around them, others wanted to seek to understand how and why the activities were taking shape, while others were more comfortable observing from a distance. Yet other children wanted to talk through their experiences in detail and share their thoughts on what was unfolding around them and what they were a part of creating.

Different modes afforded different kinds of opportunities for exploring ideas. For example, the musician in the local theatre group, created different atmospheres through various rhythmic and harmonic musical notes that set the mood for different elements of children's role play, whether it be to create mystery or stimulate energy and dancing.

Play provided opportunity to pose and explore propositions about children's local worlds. Tracey drew this example:

One day, there was the magic carpet ride and the children had landed somewhere. The children had decided, 'Let's go to the beach', and they got there. 'And now what?' There was this moment . . . One of the performers could see that the children were a bit lost, so he just jumped in a box, sat in there and started saying, 'Ice-creams! ice-creams!' And he became an ice-cream shop and he only had three or four little things in the box, like a car or a block. So children started to line up for an ice-cream and he'd say, 'What flavour?' and he'd give them the little toy car and say 'Here you are!' And the children, they'd realise that he probably only had two or three things in his box. So, they'd walk around the back and drop it in the back for him, so he'd have it for the next child. Nothing was said, nothing planned in that way. You know, he was really able to interpret, 'What's going on here?' The children had really lost their way with the narrative and were not sure where to take it, so he'd just spontaneously go over and say 'Ice-creams! Ice-creams!'

This example hearkens back to an earlier point about exploring propositions that children present through their play and interactions with others – in exploring such propositions and watching children closely, we come to see what is important to them. In this ice-cream scenario, for example, children revealed values of working together, tuning in to others, sharing materials, and seeing the possibilities and the limitations (e.g. ice-cream props running out) and working with them. These themes, inherent in children's actions, signify much about what is important to these children in their community lives.

To consider another example, trust, exploring possibility and taking risk were all apparent in the scenario of two children making a box walk. The children had covered themselves with a box lifted over their head and body with their feet sticking out the bottom. As there were no holes in the box the children couldn't see out ahead of them but could see each other and trusted each other to co-ordinate themselves to create a 'walking box'.

Through the development of ideas and imagination children were able to themselves lead their own play and explore possibilities, with adults providing new ideas as stimuli or provoking further thought if required, cautious however of not interfering with the children's own development of ideas.

As the theatre's artistic director commented of young children:

> They're at a stage of development where their ideas and their imaginations are developing and unfolding, so if we facilitate and lead their play, then they kind of take that . . . to the next level and then we can throw more ideas in the mix.

Play is children's work – it is also seen in this Western Adelaide encounter to be a vital way that children can exercise and express their active citizenship when engaging in consultations. It is for the reflective, watchful observer and listener, however, to see with all their senses what children are doing and what they are conveying in that play – what, for example, play at this Western Adelaide centre tells us about these children's sense of their communities and what's important to them in their lives, now and in the future. For example, Tracey observed:

> One of the things that I did notice . . . was some children were very busy building things with their boxes. A couple of the boys just got in a box each and just closed the door and just stayed there. When I talked to staff later, they said that both of those children came from very difficult home situations and had had quite a lot of trauma in their lives. So it made sense – they got into their box and it was as if to say: 'I'm safe and I'm staying in my space.' In that way children were able to engage, in terms of what worked for them in the experiences that were set up.

That said, staff reflected on the structures and routines that can constrain rather than enable dialogic engagement in play spaces:

> There was music and movement that facilitated children's engagement, children with deep communication issues, but it was really drama that the children hooked right into. I don't think we pay enough respect to that in our centres. I think we get a bit busy doing other things and we forget about how important this is.

So it was that these Western Adelaide children conveyed to their educators what was important to them in their day-to-day lives – not just by what they said but how they engaged with the spaces and provocations provided them. The children responded in a variety of ways:

> Some children were hysterical; there was great enjoyment and sense of the funny. They didn't always know how to deal with the unexpected, like when the actors did different things, like the actor sitting in a box and the children see this finger coming out of the box ... Some children observed, they moved closer to the action. Others showed surprise that the room was set up differently and the way the adults were engaging. Children were not familiar with action. Children really engaged with each of the performers and they flocked to and adored the open-ended activities.

This engagement saw staff re-think and affirm their own roles:

> The teacher's role is not about standing around and supervising and not being distracted by the next activity like mat time. We're not actually getting children to that deeper level of playing when we keep stopping them.

Key structural considerations that came into play related to organisation, time, continuity and considering the needs of the children. As previously noted, staff reduced the size of groups, to hear children's voices, and to also ensure that what unfolded was indeed collaborative – a matter of 'we'. Setting up the space for the actors and children to interact with each other worked well by all reports, as did allowing children to choose the experiences in which they would like to be involved.

Staff saw that not only were the performers free from preconceptions of children that can see adults limit children's participation. The performers were also free from 'having to think about routines, such as morning tea time or setting up different activities' ... as an early childhood educator at the centre remarked: 'I looked at it just going, "Wow, this says so much about the way we work and maybe about the way we need to re-think some of the things about the way we work."'

100 Music, drama and play in a Western Adelaide community

Inherent in such considerations are tensions related to relative power and exercise of authority in dialogic encounters such as these consultations, as Tracey commented:

> One of the other things that I did notice that was quite interesting was how disrupted children's play can be by routine times. So when they had to stop when they were deeply engaged in really deep dramatic play, and then someone would say, 'It's morning tea!' They just did not want to go, but they had to, they had no choice about it. So I thought that was an interesting thing in terms of thinking about children's voice. Do we hear it? Or is it more about convenience of what we need to do? Because the children were really deeply engaged in what was going on.

The depth of children's prolonged engagement was notable to all who observed, and marked a shift from previous encounters outside this dialogic, multi-modal consultative space. For example, the centre's cook witnessed the children's involvement, the intensity of their concentration and the depth and breadth of their responses:

> The cook's positioned in the kitchen in the middle of the centre and sees everything that is going on. She was amazed that children who never draw, at the end of the first day, children who never draw, avoid it altogether and would rather be outside riding bikes or whatever – after being involved in that dramatic play on the first day, they wanted to sit down and draw and talk about their experience of what they'd just done. And the cook said, 'This should be happening all the time.'

Observations like this saw educators and performers critically reflect on how teaching and children's learning takes place:

> I wonder whether we spend enough time doing this stuff with children, this kind of work using music, movement, song and things in this kind of way or whether we just do it as an add-on? Or a bit here or there or whether we integrate it in this way to really get children's creative thinking and narrative happening? How much do we value this? Have we allowed things like literacy and numeracy in a very formal sense to push this kind of really important work to the edges of that work instead of making it central? So to me, that was probably one of the biggest lessons for me in sitting back and watching how the children engaged ... One of the challenges for us is to really look at what is getting in the way, do we value creativity and the arts and play and if we do then how do we make it that it can happen.
>
> (Tracey)

It really is the adult's responsibility to create an environment that has many options. It can still be a safe place but within that there can be many options.

(One of the performers)

Educators linked children's engagement to EYLF's themes of belonging, being and becoming, as Tracey explained:

Belonging and connectedness were exemplified through the group and coming together and building a house, building houses together. Children tried out new ideas trying out new roles, different possibilities. The 'Being' was a huge one because, I think, this whole strategy revolved around *being* with children and engaging with children. And the children were absolutely delighted when adults were willing to be with them and go where they wanted to go, instead of saying, 'Well, we've got to go onto something else.' The notion of becoming and 'What's the next thing?' – the next developmental step for children or getting ready for school . . . You can really tune into belonging, being and becoming, not as separate things but altogether, moment to moment.

Children's themes

Children's comments during play revealed key themes important to them – for example, connectedness and separateness through putting boxes together and pulling them apart, resonant with people coming together and coming apart. Children's sense of the changeability of reality also came through, as Tracey described when they 'created their environment and then pulled it apart and created it differently again. I think is a really key thing that children were showing was important to them and they enjoyed it.'

In this kind of engagement, children saw and played with possibility. Possibilities like:

Safe scary . . . darkness, baddies, scary hose monsters. Feeling safe in a kindergarten environment. Children like to feel that thrill and excitement of danger and risk in using the props in particular narratives. Having an opportunity for them to experience or express feelings of being scared and frightened in that way which I think has a really clear message for us about the way we make our centres so safe and our environment so safe, that children don't have those opportunities.

Animals and pets, gardens, trees and flowers, fruit and vegetables, emerged as more material themes. So did a sustainable environment: 'If we don't look after the trees, we'll all be dead' – a more frightening proposition than the 'safe scary' ideas children expressed.

102 Music, drama and play in a Western Adelaide community

Educators and the theatre group created two DVDs (further described in Chapter 8). One of these DVDs documented children's themes through a digital animation, put together by children themselves after being provided some guidance on using the computer software, accompanied by children's commentary. The DVD explores children's favourite places and spaces, as well as places they wouldn't like to live in, with imagination and reality entwined to paint a poignant picture of children's views about their world.

On many occasions children expressed their desires through fantasy and imagination, then linking those concepts to analogous situations in their real world. Quentin, for example, identified the cemetery as being his favourite place which at first would appear to an adult as a strange place for a child to identify in a favourable light. However, by listening further to Quentin's views, it became clear that he usually didn't like cemeteries and found them scary. However, he liked the particular cemetery he had created through his animation. Rather than being a scary and dark place, he had made it colourful, bright and less confronting, thus bringing to life possibilities for the way adults design spaces that children as well as adults visit.

Likewise Jordan linked concepts based on fantasy to practical considerations in the real world. He stated:

> Hello I'm Jordan. I have made up a tent island. It's full of giant people. They are protecting the island and its treasure. I think it is important to protect the environment to keep it clean and safe. In this scene Alice and Ben is getting married. They are getting married in a beautiful place filled with flowers and a nice shaded area. There is no places like that where I live. I wish there was.

Similarly, Natasha linked concepts explored through an imaginary world to her real life desires, stating:

> This is a place where I wouldn't like to live. I could get eaten by the T-Rex and the Mummies are scary. Another place that is scary is the park near my house. There are giant slides and they look really scary. They should have smaller slides for littler kids.

Maria also linked an imaginary ballroom with a prince and a princess to her love of dancing, providing insight through role-play of what she enjoys in terms of real life possibilities. Likewise Tanya linked the North Pole with her love of toy hunts and her dog Ruby.

In many instances, children expressed their views by directly linking their thoughts to the real world rather than making analogies through fantasy and imagination. Quentin, for example, identified his dislike of drunk drivers, making roads unsafe. Oscar identified his love of the sea, fishing and swimming and a desire to learn to scuba dive.

Zara identified her love of the classroom and school and her wish for her classroom to be more colourful. She also said she liked to spend time with friends and dancing at the RSL with her mum, once again expressing her desire for colourful decorations. She expressed her love for singing, music, the beach, turtles and fish.

In a similar manner, based on real -life experiences Patsy stated:

> Hi my name's Patsy. My favourite place is a big space with a big playground. It has flowers and a rainbow because it looks pretty. I like it here because I can play chasey and hide and seek. I made another place too. This one is a river with dirt and garbage. I don't like this place because it is no good when people want to go fishing and they will only catch food and rubbish. I wish people would be tidier.

The children also regularly expressed concern for community and social issues as well as the environment. This is evident from the examples provided already such as concern of drunk drivers and of litter or pollution. Further examples are provided by Gail who identified a need for more swimming pools to be enjoyed by all in her community. Maria expressed a dislike of litter and offered a possible solution of more bins being publicly available to people. Likewise Nicky identified a love of the outdoors, animals and parks.

Reflecting on the Western Adelaide case study

The magic carpet ride that began this encounter serves as an apt metaphor of empowerment, realised through the power of imaginary and exploratory play and dialogue. In this play, in which adults joined children as co-players and co-constructors, children reframed their perspectives of 'kindy' and their local community at large. In this re-framing, children expressed themselves in relation to others in their world. They sought and found new possibilities in their reality that became transformed through their engagement in and reflection about their world – as the theatre group director found:

> [And] what we found over the four days of exploring with these young children was that they wanted to construct their own world and they didn't need to have kind of solid formal materials, the cardboard boxes they were able to turn into whatever shape, form or environment that they could think of that suited their creative journey at that particular moment. They could flatten it, they could open it out, they could climb in it, they could climb under it, they could pack it away, bring it in, put it together and create a little city out of it if they wanted to. And that seems to be what's lacking in their world in terms of how we've formalised it, that we create the play equipment. We shape it and they just use it, so . . . it's not a co-constructed process where they actually get to make it themselves and make it according to the

feeling and thought and the emotion of the journey that they want to go on at this particular point in time.

Transformation pervaded the entire encounter – an empowering process of re-imagining, with children becoming immersed in the characters within their role play, their ideas valued within the spaces they themselves took ownership in creating as four-year-olds, with the promise of opportunity and possibilities for the future – capturing the very essence of belonging, being and becoming as promoted through the EYLF.

The design of the encounter afforded opportunities to unleash children's capacity for re-imagining themselves and their external reality. As one of the performers put it: 'It became an empowerment, that's what a lot of the design really was aimed at.'

With empowerment, however, comes risk, for adults and children alike, as an educator at this Western Adelaide centre found and remarked to Tracey:

> One of the staff said, 'I don't want to pre-empt anybody here.' I think she was worried about whether she should step back or be vigilant so things didn't get out of hand, you know, with children who are particularly complex. But then as it happened and she saw, and we're talking about a child who had quite complex behaviours, he took a lead role and he was great and totally engaged with it.

In taking risk to be empowered and to empower others, discretionary judgment and tuning in to children with all one's senses are critical, as the performers themselves showed:

> The performers were responsive to what children needed and stepped in to continue a narrative with the children. They saw the big picture – the themes, the assembling and disassembling. They saw what the children were doing with the boxes and chairs, putting things together, what they were creating, what the children were doing with the props.
>
> (Tracey)

The performers saw these actions and the deeper meanings or possibilities they signified – and the performers engaged *in simpatico*. In turn, this engagement validated children's ongoing participation. As the children became accustomed to their new space, educators noted that the children became 'so excited, they wanted to come every day ... The children were just so enthusiastic and everyday were saying, "Are you coming back? Are you coming back?"' One particular child most potently expressed renewed enthusiasm to participate:

At the end of the day, there was this little guy who the staff had said had 'huge communication issues'. He was lying on the lounge and he called out to the performers as they were leaving for the day, 'That was the best day ever! I hope you are coming back!'

Chapter 8

Authentically documenting children's messages

We wanted to make sure we didn't put adult speak on what the children were saying.

(Educator in the Children's Voices Project)

In the Children's Voices Project, educators experienced a newfound professional freedom, indeed permission, to take the time necessary and innovate on their practices as the situation demanded – as the previous case study chapters have richly illustrated. At the same time, these encounters compelled educators to think carefully about how they were engaging with children's voices and how they would be accountable to government – and how therefore they would document children's messages in authentic ways that 'rang true' with what children expressed.

In the Children's Voices Project, authentic documentation involved recording children's voices accurately and clearly, assisted in various ways across the sites by photography, audio- and video-recordings, and running and anecdotal records. Authentic documentation also meant checking it was valid – that is, true to the meaning and intent of what children expressed, cross-checked with those who know the child and, most importantly, the child him- or herself – as seen in the previous case study chapters.

Contextualising what children expressed also was important to authentic documentation and understanding children's meaning and intent – especially when what children expressed is lifted out of its immediate context and conveyed to someone else such as the government. In the case studies we have explored, educators' final reports to government provided accounts of their operational contexts and how they approached the consultations in their particular site.

Authentic documentation of children's voices needs to have clarity, allowing valid extrapolations to be made about broader thematic interests and concerns that children's messages may represent – with opportunity to cross-check these extrapolations with our key informants.

Clarity can be challenged by the complexity inherent in children's messages expressed through multiple modes. Capturing complexity involves showing depth and breadth of children's meaning in what children express, and doing justice to such meaning when representing it to an external audience. For a

Authentically documenting children's messages   107

government agency audience, documentation needs to distil key messages clearly to inform future policy directions.

Finally, authentic documentation does not put 'adult speak' on what children express – it is true to the voice of the child and includes where appropriate the actual words of what children say, signifying their broader thematic interests (after Freire, 1983).

Let us now re-visit our four case study sites from Chapters 4 to 7 and consider how the educators in each site documented the consultations, before we then consider educators' collective reflections on authentically documenting children's views.

Documenting the encounter at the four case study sites

Limestone Town kindergarten and rural care

In this service, educators were explicit with children about the purpose of and means for documenting what children said, as the educators had planned:

> We let children know we really valued and wanted to hear what they thought about their community . . . We explained to each child that we would be writing down what they said as this was a really important thing they were telling us . . . We consistently recognised and encouraged the children through discussion and feedback . . . We were also very aware of how we documented children's voices respectfully . . . We worked to keep true to what the children said.

Educators' documentation was informed by observing and listening to children, becoming researchers of and with the children:

> We would watch what the children enjoyed doing at the centre. We used our knowledge of that child from observations of photos and work samples. We also enlisted the help of the parents and asked them what their child was doing and the places they liked to visit. We felt that by doing this, we'd be able to capture the children's own voice. We wanted to make sure that the ideas were authentic.

Authenticity was a firm underpinning of this encounter that required ongoing vigilance:

> I felt that this project was about the children's work and I was having to stop myself occasionally with other staff, not to put words into their mouth. . . .
> I think that was what the project was about, actually maintaining the children's voice. We were quite adamant that we would try not to put words

108 Authentically documenting children's messages

in children's mouths. We didn't make any interpretations at all. We wrote the children's stories about their artwork word-for-word.

In working to ensure high-fidelity documentation to make children's insights visible and their voices heard, educators continued to cross-check their records with the children:

> The final product was where we actually went back and quietly got the child, and we took a photo of them and their artwork. We then asked them, 'Tell us about your painting.' And so we just wrote word-for-word exactly what they had done. Here's an example – these are the words of one of the children. [Reading from the documentation] 'I like being in the shed. We made the broom. The wool gets sold to the market and then it goes to the factory. Then you make socks out of it. There are shearer men, they take it into Limestone Town.'

Educators' focus with 'maintaining the voice of the children and what they wanted to do' extended to how the artists engaged with the children:

> We didn't really want to let the artist have total control. We wanted to keep the whole thing at what the children wanted to do and asking them. Making sure the children did what they wanted to do on the final work. We were adamant to maintain the children's voices for their final art work.

The final report for DECS was compiled as a substantial ring folder containing information about the site's context, including: photos of Limestone Town; their planning document; descriptions of their consultation strategies and the central theme they used to implement their strategy; observational accounts and photographs of the interactions and experiences throughout the encounter, including working with the two visiting artists; recording sheets of conversations with individual children; children's themes that emerged; and individual children's artefacts and photos of their artistic creations.

Educators were candid about the challenge they faced in making interpretations *with* and not *for* the child:

> There may have been some possible interpretations when it came to producing the artwork. That was probably the hardest thing because I have an art background in print-making. I just had to be careful not to try and put too many ideas in. We talked with children and provided them with resources to choose to use – like different coloured papers for a rainbow. Leaving the child to do the art himself. Helping a child to find what he wanted. Going for a walk around the centre to find the kind of rubbish he wanted to put on his artwork [about litter]. So that was probably the thing, trying to maintain the integrity and the voice of the child.

Home learning partnership programme in the Eyre and Western Region

With cameras in children's hands and children choosing what to photograph and how, their views of their local worlds came through with clear and compelling authenticity. Children's photographs revealed what they really liked and were passionate about – and more, gave all who viewed the photos a sense of what it is like to be in that child's shoes and looking at the world through their lens.

When it came to documenting the final report for DECS, more time was taken for deciding how to go about this task. Nicola explained her deliberations this way:

> I had to stop and think about it for a little bit initially. I wasn't sure how much I needed to write . . . I just sort of sat down, scribbled it out and thought, 'OK, this is what I roughly need to do.' I thought I needed to say a little bit about the children's lives, where they live . . . and whoever is important to them in their lives . . . Then I talked about the children and what they enjoyed. So once I got my head around that, I found it not too hard and followed through . . . Comments about children's photographs were written in relationship to what the teacher knew that the child liked if the child didn't have the language to express it themselves. On a particular day, comments were written about what the child liked if the child brought a toy to the teacher, through their own action – that connection with the teacher and the child formed the basis of the communication.

The final report was compiled as a display folder containing descriptions of the site's context and consultation theme, strategy and online resources; and individual profiles of each child's context and background, interests and photos (as prints, small photocopies and CD). Parents and children together decided what photographs were included in the report sent to DECS.

The report also included children's posters. In collaboration with parents and educators, each child collated his/her own photos in a poster. Children made their own selections for their particular posters, talked the photos through with their parents and educators, and provided captions that adults scribed. Adults also capitalised on children's non-verbal cues to inform these captions – recognising children's verbal and non-verbal capabilities.

Out-of-school-hours care service in the Fleurieu Peninsula and Kangaroo Island Region

Educators at this Fleurieu OSHC service documented the entire dialogic encounter through their planning documents and related artefacts (posters, invitations and letters); photographs, observational records and on-the-spot recordings of children's interactions; collection of children's draft drawings and captions; and the wall hanging itself, accompanied by a written group statement

110 Authentically documenting children's messages

about what children wished for in their lives. This documentation was collated as a comprehensive and quite detailed final report in a spiral-bound book.

Tuning into children's views, educators asked children questions about their drawings and actively listened to and documented *verbatim* what children expressed, as explained by educators and evidenced in their final report:

> We didn't interpret. We wrote directly what was said, documented how it was heard and said. With some children, the teacher did not understand their explanations around their art but it was still recorded as said. If further clarification was needed, more questions were asked. This meant teachers developed a clear understanding. Some children could write their explanations themselves.

Educators' individual conversations with children about their drawings were critical to the authenticity of the dialogic process:

> It was important we talked with each child to find out what the child's picture meant – get them to describe that picture. Children told the teachers about their own choices to include certain things in their artwork, and linked their pictures to their ideas. The child's own words are important for people to know what the child's picture means, their understanding and their interpretations. It's important to have the words so adults understand what the child means. Government people can't interpret a child's picture unless they know from the child what it means.

The importance of the children's words and the broader thematic concerns they represented was potently illustrated in a child's drawing of a rocket ship taking off into space, flames pouring out of its jets:

> It's just a picture of a rocket ship with a flame coming out of the bottom. If you were to look at that in any context, you would interpret it in your own way. But I'd like to give you Ethan's interpretation of that rocket picture. [Reading the child's words] 'I wish everyone a healthy and happy community, that is a community that is eco friendly, an environment that is well looked after where we protect all animals and endangered species. I will be happy, helpful and healthy when looking after my community. My space station will be able to view all the planets in the solar system to make sure they are eco friendly.'

The possibility of multiple interpretations gave pause for these educators to reflect on

> how we, the teachers, interpret a child's message and how the children interpret what we want. More than one staff could interpret children's work in different ways – because of telling the child what they are seeing in the

picture. The questioning needs to be done by one person using the same questions so that it is consistent and the child's views are given, not the views of the teacher or childcare worker.

Educators found what they described as 'a massive difference in response as far as children's artistic ability is concerned', further reinforcing educators' views about interpretation:

> So it's not about artistic ability and what they put in the picture. It's about the understanding of what the picture meant in terms of how the child, understood what is important to them in the future. If the children weren't artistic, their reflection was. Their reflection on their drawing was great as they wanted to explain the bits in their pictures and why they've added them. Reflection is important for children.

Reflection is important indeed to authentically documenting children's words and voices, and to coming to understand what these words personally signify in dialogue with others. In the focus here on children's reflection on their pieces of work, we see action (the children's drawings) coming together with reflection (what children said their drawings signified in terms of what was important to them now and in the future) – the genesis of what Freire (1983) defines as praxis – the dialectic between reflection and action. Indeed, a next step in this encounter with children in this Fleurieu OSHC service, beyond the remit of these particular consultations, could be thinking about further action children might plan and take in response to their reflections.

According to the educators and as evidenced in their extensive and quite detailed final report, 'a lot of time was spent on putting the documentation together. There were lots of examples that we included. Everything's got Why? When? Where? Who did what and how it was done?'

The final report was compiled as a spiral-bound book containing information about the approach to the consultations, how the consultations were framed, planned, implemented and documented; photographs taken throughout the encounter; individual children's original drawings and captions; a synthesis statement co-constructed with the children to capture recurring themes within the group; and a photo of the collation of all the children's works as a 'What do you wish for?' wall hanging.

Children's centre and out-of-school-hours care in the Western Adelaide Region

Educators at this Western Adelaide centre maintained observational records of what the performers did and how the children engaged, describing their actions, reactions, the things they said and expressed. Photographs and video-recordings were also made. In the documentation that took place, educators' focus on 'small

112 Authentically documenting children's messages

skills and details' stood in contrast to performers' open-ended, creative planning informed by seeing children's 'big picture ideas, their themes'.

Thus the documentation needed to capture these themes even as they unfolded and be the source of ongoing reflection and planning. Educators shared insights into what they saw in terms of what they knew about the children; film-makers looked at the film and talked about what they were seeing and what they were hearing children say; and the performers talked about their experience with the children and what they were seeing and hearing. These reflections occurred at the end of each day.

Through these documented means, based on some intensive explorations previously described, children showed what was important to them in authentic ways that were true to children's intentions and desires. As Tracey remarked:

> We need to know about the children and what they have to say, so they tell us, instead of us setting up something for children to say it in a certain way.

Staff and the theatre group created two DVDs. One documented children's involvement in music, movement, drama, painting, drawing and dramatic play and particularly documented adults' experiences of the process from a distance to not distract or detract from children's experiences. The other DVD documented children's themes through a digital animation, put together by children themselves after being provided some guidance on using the computer software, accompanied by children's commentary.

This second DVD provided valuable insights into children's thoughts and views with resonating evidence of the links children made between imagination, themes explored during their role playing and significant issues for them in their real life communities. This made strikingly evident the insightful observations of one of the performers that we as adults need to put aside the 'preconceived ideas' of what children are expressing and instead focus on 'just taking time to listen to the child' – as through listening is the only way to truly understand.

The DVD explores children's favourite places and spaces as well as places they wouldn't like to live in with imagination and reality intricately intertwining to paint a poignant picture of children's views about their world.

Educators' reflections on authentically documenting children's views

Authentic documentation validates the child and his or her participation. This validation was not lost on children. Educators observed children's own sense of validation from being involved in these government consultations:

> It was lovely for [the children] to know that their voice was really important. Children were proud of what they were doing . . . We were hearing children in the garden after we'd been talking about places in our community. They

were talking about, 'Have you been to the park with the big slide?' and things like that . . . initiating conversation between each other as well which was lovely, and comparing their stories they had shared in the consultations.

At the outset of the Children's Voices Project, guidance regarding documentation was provided to educators undertaking the consultations with children in both the induction materials and induction workshop. This guidance emphasised the importance of documentation from planning to final reporting, which would involve visible, active listening to children.

While this guidance was provided, there was flexibility in how educators chose to present their documentation in ways that suited their contexts and the consultation strategies they used. Consequently, ways in which educators documented their children's consultations were diverse but equally effective.

Documentation involved educators carefully considering how they were going to accurately record what children were saying at given moments and in particular situations. Some educators recorded 'snippets' around observations, while others developed a recording format. Some recorded on post-it notes or in a notebook as they talked with children, making sure that this documentation focused on the children's words.

Educators worked to remain true to the integrity of children's voices and words through a variety of strategies, such as helping children to express themselves through further questioning, paraphrasing what children might mean, and checking educators' interpretations with children throughout the process. Clarification with children and breaking down questions for ease of understanding all contributed to educators' attempts to maintain children's voices without placing their own interpretations on what was seen or observed.

How educators talked about this aspect of the consultations revealed the conscious effort it took to step out of the way of children's voices. Engaging with children on a one-to-one basis and in small groups facilitated authentic documentation. Educators and children alike were impressed with the time they spent with children on an individual basis in terms of the discussions that evolved as a result of individual attention. As one educator put it: 'Actually having that luxury of being able to sit down for long periods of time and just talk to the children made it really good to get a clearer idea of what they want.' Educators found their discussions with children deepened as a result, and they became more aware of listening to children and valuing what they say.

Educators' awareness of their documentation practices was also heightened in consequence of this experience, appreciating the significance of children's words and the broader themes they represent. They wrote word-for-word what children said, and video-recording provided a means to review children's participation and what they said. As an educator explained:

I'd ask some questions, then ask the children then to do a drawing. As they were drawing, I would just write down everything they said. I'd ask them some questions, and seek some clarification, and write down what came out of the answers.

Capturing children's words was a challenge but one that educators valued. For example:

> I was trying not to put my thoughts into the documentation. I was trying just to write what the children had said to me. The questions that were in the briefing, I just used those questions and then tried not to think of my own formula to answer the questions. I just let children answer as they would and then wrote those straight as I got them . . . I tried not to put anything of myself into it, just what the children said. I tried not to make my own interpretations.

Educators valued and needed children's words to assist in their own interpretations, sensing there was deeper meaning to explore in children's talk and creations that connected with the core themes of what mattered to children and what children wished for in their lives. For example, one educator commented:

> The challenge was making sure that the words were truly the children's, and not what I was interpreting. I did lots of thinking as I was writing. I was writing up about what was their true intent and trying to remember what exactly the words that they used. It was hard to hear sometimes if it was noisy, so that was a challenge. I needed to make sure that I was hearing what they were saying, and not the expectations that would affect my hearing of what they were saying. Repetition of what children said about what they liked or didn't like doing helped. When the children came up with the same responses week after week, I felt comfortable with saying: 'Well you know that's what they really value that because they keep repeating that.'

Capturing children's intent saw educators cross-check with their colleagues, children's families and their ultimate informants, the children themselves. As one educator remarked, 'You might have thought that the children had forgotten what they had said or done in their thought processes, but they didn't. They remembered.' Another educator explained:

> I would ask the children if I was unsure. I'd say, 'You're talking about the big slide at the playground, is that the curly slide there?' And they'd say, 'No, that's the whatever.' Things like that, talking around what they were actually drawing. 'Is that a person there?' 'Is that the person there that you have drawn for me?' 'I'm going to write some things on your paper now. Is that ok?' 'What would you like me to write?' 'What do you want me to write under this picture?' Making sure that I was labelling it correctly.

Observing children's conversations with one another also provided more impromptu and quite ongoing ways of checking validity of what an educator was recording.

Collegial support was deeply valued and much needed in this encounter:

> The beauty of working in a staff team is that usually, if you get it wrong, then somebody else has heard, and they get it right, so that's the thing.

As noted in the previous case study chapters, it was not simply a matter of what children said or did in direct response to questions that were posed – it was in the processes of their engagement that much was revealed and therefore documented about what children saw made life valuable.

Children's own sense of validation grew from being listened to and their words and actions carefully noted:

> It was valuable to be able to concentrate on small groups, it made it really good for getting a clearer idea of what children want. It was good for me and it was good for the children. And for some of the children, it was really good for their confidence to be able to sit down and talk about the things that were important to them, and not feel rushed or hurried, and to feel that I was really listening, they had all my attention.

One documentation strategy that was found to be unsuccessful was video-recording children being interviewed on camera. The educators choosing this technique quickly came to see this created a situation that was confronting for the children and distorted the relationship between child and educator, and reduced children's comfort and sense of freedom in expressing their ideas. Consequently the camera interview idea was abandoned.

The careful approach educators took to listening to children and documenting their words and actions extended to the educators' final reports they prepared for DECS:

> When I put the [final documentation] together, sometimes I edited because the children would often get off track onto other things. I tried not to take too much of it out because I wanted to keep it true to what the children were saying. But if the children went off into a little spiel about something, like there was someone throwing sand in the sand pit, I didn't put that in because it was totally something different. I tried to keep the conversations around the drawing and the events that they were trying to portray through the drawings . . . I wanted to get the children's answers, not what I expected or not what they thought I wanted them to say. I wanted children's true feelings rather than them thinking, 'What does she want me to do here?'

While educators had been guided by principles of authentic documentation and the ways they were accustomed to documenting children's experiences in their programmes, educators would have preferred more guidance in how to approach and write up the final documentation to be given to DECS in a way that met DECS' requirements and would be effective in informing policy decisions. Educators' uncertainties included presentation style and how much information to include in the final report. These uncertainties led educators to develop their own appropriate frameworks and, in consequence, each final report was quite unique, as illustrated in the earlier case study chapters.

In some cases, educators edited their final reports several times and revisited their records to review what children had expressed. Educators in the main felt it was important to ensure that their final documentation was 'reader friendly' for the audience. Support from the project's planning team was seen to be important and valued by educators in assisting with the production of the final documentation.

Another documentation challenge related to educators implementing their day-to-day programmes and sustaining ongoing interruptions while implementing the consultations. Allocating staff to observe and document the process meant that other staff needed to take carriage of other aspects of the centre's programme and those children not involved in the consultations. Being mindful of the time spent and finding the right time to document the consultations were significant challenges for educators. Listening to children in a noisy environment also provided challenges around accurately hearing what children had said. One educator explained:

> Part of the problem in our kind of work is, because it's so noisy and there's so much happening and all the rest of it, that you're just moving around groups of children only interacting for a very short period of time before you are moving around the next group to intervene or whatever. So you're not actually for a lot of the time hearing what they're saying sometimes. You think you are responding to their needs but in actual fact you haven't actually really seen them . . . Stronger willed, confident children will say 'No . . . . I want so and so' or 'No . . .' but there's a lot of children who don't, so they miss out because you haven't heard.

In some centres, there was a problem with lack of resources that provided some challenges. Time spent on the final product was quite substantial in some cases. In one case educators used their home resources to print coloured photos and compile their documentation. Assistance from the project's planning group was subsequently provided for their final printing and binding. Implications for future projects mean that this aspect of the process needs to be more carefully work-shopped and resourced.

Educators' reflections on doing things differently next time related to the gathering of more data. Suggested changes included exploring children's art works more deeply with them, and using voice recorders to document children's interactions. Access to these recorders was seen as invaluable so educators could check what children actually said in the conversation process, rather than just relying on their notes. As one educator identified 'for accurate recording of children responses . . . We could play it back when it was quieter and check that our writing was correct and that assumptions weren't being made.' Referring to video footage as a way of documenting was also recommended as a possible way to gain data and document in future projects. While identified earlier that interviewing children on camera was found not to be a successful technique, taking video footage of activities from a distance was found to work successfully.

Overall there was consensus that up to this point in the process there had been great success in implementing the consultations with children and documenting their thoughts, views and desires. However, the wealth of information that educators provided presented another difficult, yet equally rewarding challenge – how to meaningfully analyse, interpret and synthesise children's messages in a way that would influence public policy directions. A recount of this next stage of the Children's Voices Project – developing a DECS report for DPC – is explored in the following chapter.

Chapter 9

Reporting and uptake of children's messages

The way we got the information from DECS was really clear. I mean it was still in children's own words and it's still their ideas, but it was really clear ... I use the words, 'the honesty of the process'.

(DPC's Manager of Community Engagement and
Consultations for the State Strategic Plan)

The greater the accountability of government authorities is to children whose participation they have sought, the greater the respect and recognition of children's citizenship and views. Inherent in such accountability is transparency of purpose and outcomes of children's participation. The process of consulting itself is a valuable means of supporting children's sense of citizenship and democracy as well as leading by example to demonstrate to disengaged adults the importance of recognising children as citizens and empowering their participation.

However, if the process is wrapped up and considered a success once the consultation activity with children has been completed and their words and creations have been shared, then children's participation is devalued and so, too, is their sense of citizenship and desire to so engage again. Involving children meaningfully in consultations requires a commitment to taking time to interpret and understand children's views and to translate these views into meaningful action as an outcome of a collaborative decision-making process.

The South Australian Children's Voices Project had the strength of bringing together educators and children with policymakers and a researcher, each bringing their individual expertise to produce meaningful outcomes. Even so, the data produced at the conclusion of the consultations with children were both rich and overwhelming. The data needed to be respectfully organised, analysed and interpreted to ensure children's views were reflected, while balancing the need for those views to be presented in a style to which policymakers were accustomed and most likely to act upon. So doing posed key challenges involved in managing the representation of children's voices and disseminating findings (Wise, 2009).

Making sense of the data

Once educators' final reports were provided to DECS, the next step was for DECS staff to analyse this information. As the Senior Policy Adviser (Manatakis) co-ordinating the Children's Voices Project reported:

> Staff wanted to make sure that in their analysis and interpreting of this information, they didn't put adult speak or adult interpretations onto the information received that related to what the children were saying. In order to retain the authenticity of the children's voice, the DECS team, with their range of expertise, came together and looked at each individual statement from the children and grouped that into various themes . . . People in DECS from different backgrounds talked about each individual child's opinion and worked through what each child said and how that fitted into themes which were similar to what other children were saying.

The data generated at each of the sites participating in the Children's Voices Project took various forms, as illustrated in the case study chapters in this book. Children's artistic and creative expression, such as their paintings, drawings and photos, as well as the written documentation of children's spoken expression, were all included. As this information came from a range of consultations using different strategies, inconsistencies in the way in which children's voices were captured required a consistent approach to analysing and synthesising all children's views in a logical and easy-to- understand format.

As a starting point, a small team of four people come together to commence organising the information. It was essential the people involved in this stage brought to the table a diverse range of expertise from across the fields of research, policy and practice. Thus this team included the de Lissa Chair in Early Childhood Research (Harris), the Senior Policy Adviser co-ordinating the consultation project (Manatakis) and the Early Childhood Adviser (Tracey) contributing to the project's planning and who worked directly with some of the educators and children in undertaking the consultations. This team approach provided a sharing of expertise among those skilled in working with children, as well as linking those responsible for translating children's voices into action through public policy.

Thematisation – that is, grouping children's messages according to topics that emerged from the children's data – was the approach taken to analysis. This process involved going though each piece of data and discussing as a group the meaning of children's expression. Seeking to understand children's underlying messages was essential to ensuring children's authentic voices continued to be reflected in this next stage of the Children's Voices Project. Educators' documentation provided insight for this interpretive work.

Doing this work as a small team allowed colleagues to cross-check their analysis and interpretation with one another, ensuring greater consistency in interpretation. Ultimately, the Senior Policy Adviser (Manatakis) took carriage of this work.

120   Reporting and uptake of children's messages

A matrix was developed with the emergent themes going across the table, with sub-themes clustered beneath each broader theme where required. Key ideas associated with each theme or sub-themes were entered in the table's cells, colour-coded so each idea could be tracked to the service from whence it came. This tracking provided a sense of distribution of and consensus among children's ideas within and across regions. Positive and negative comments were delineated by '+' and '−' respectively; and the counts of comments represented a count by consultation not by child. A count by child was not included due to the different documentation methods of each consultation. In the face of these inconsistencies, a count by child would have distorted a sense of data terms and thus create reliability issues.

Generating these themes created an initial tension among DECS staff as they were concerned that they might be imposing their own frames of reference on children's input. However, once emergent thematisation techniques, well established in the literature (e.g. Corbin and Strauss, 2008; Glesne, 2006), were explored, staff were reassured in generating themes in ways that stayed true to the children's data. Moreover, as the Senior Policy Adviser further explained in his interview, DECS staff wished 'to make sure the Department for the Premier and Cabinet had the information presented in a meaningful way, considering that the data that came in were from 350 children . . . The intention of the DECS team was not to dilute the information.'

Reporting children's views as themes

Once the information from children had been analysed and grouped into similar categories it became possible to report on this information as themes. The themes that emerged were:

- Theme 1: The environment
- Theme 2: Family, friends and people
- Theme 3: Activities and play
- Theme 4: Animals and creatures
- Theme 5: Food
- Theme 6: Emotions and feelings
- Theme 7: Transport
- Theme 8: The future
- Theme 9: Participation.

These themes were synthesised and illustrated in the final DECS report, 'What is important to children in their communities and what do children wish for in their lives?: Report for South Australia's Strategic Plan Community Engagement Board' (Community Engagement Board, 2011) which was made available to all staff and families participating in the consultations. The report was published on DECS' website and made directly available to DPC for deliberation and uptake.

Preparing a report with these themes clearly articulated was considered to be the most valuable means of conveying to those who were to make decisions based on children's views, what it was children had expressed. Providing a summary of this information within a report was considered likely to be more useful than simply providing the raw data for interpretation, particularly for those people who are not skilled in working in partnership with children directly. At the same time it was considered important not to dilute the voices and views of individual children, the context in which issues were raised and the frequency in which individual children identified similar issues. Therefore, the final DECS report provided a detailed but succinct account of children's themes, with an appended matrix overviewing the themes and their frequencies by service. As the Senior Policy Adviser stated in a post-project interview:

> The report . . . included each of the individual things that each child had said as the original information, so that people could go back and reflect on that information if needed. That information could also be accessed in the event of future planning where people could find out the opinions of children on that subject within that data collated in the report. There was a conscious effort to ensure that the report was made reader friendly. Part of the reason for doing this was also to educate people who receive that information and may not have an understanding of Early Childhood.

In order to position the report to influence policy, some discussion of children's themes was provided in terms of the research literature at large, thereby strengthening the report's evidence as to possible impacts responding to children's thematic interests and concerns would have on children and communities. For example, if a lack of public green spaces was to arise as a common area of interest for children, this theme would be linked to relevant research and specific policy areas such as urban design, linking children's wellbeing and physical activity to public space. Explicit connections such as this to public policy and a research evidence base made appropriate consideration of children's views more likely. How this approach was put into practice with the nine themes identified by children is explained below.

Nine key themes identified by children

The environment

One of the strongest themes identified by young children was the environment. It included aspects related to both the natural environment and the built environment, with a strong sense of connection to nature. Young children identified the importance of being outdoors and in touch with nature, enjoying and discovering their surrounds and appreciating the environment. There was a strong sense of responsibility in looking after the environment and a desire for less noise and litter. Children also identified a dislike of busy locations. Large open spaces were identified as being very important and the visual beauty of nature was also a key aspect of this theme. As identified by Rose and Rosenow (2007, p. 40):

> Nature-based outdoor spaces provide a perfect setting for meeting each child's unique sensory needs. While one child may choose to quietly observe a ladybug crawling on a leaf, another child may exuberantly fill and dump pails full of sand. A wider variety of natural materials provides ways for each child to feel comfortable and successful.

Within the built environment, child-specific infrastructure such as playgrounds and preschools were identified by children as valued spaces. Of great significance too, were local landmarks such as a jetty or a lighthouse that were in children's communities that were not necessarily built with children in mind. This finding highlights the need to consider structures in urban planning from children's perspectives, even if not purpose-built with children in mind. Local structures in the community are important to children, and they engage in many such spaces with adults. There was also an importance placed on the way things are designed with a preference for lots of different textures, things that move, things that are visually appealing and colourful.

Family, friends and people

An equally strong theme related to family, friends, and people. Children placed much store in spending time with others, going places together and sharing activities. In addition to immediate family, grandparents were often identified as very important people in many children's lives. Visiting and sleeping over at family members' and friends' houses was identified as highly popular, as was spending time with parents at work. The importance of friendly neighbours within a child's community also was identified as important by some children. Others, particularly the 20 per cent of children with additional needs participating in the project, valued the professional staff they spend time with regularly, such as physiotherapists being identified as people with whom they had an ongoing connection.

In further analysing children's views, it became clear that the theme of family, friends and people tied in closely with the theme of the environment. The importance of spending time with loved ones at particular locations (whether at home or in public places) was a strong element of this theme – demonstrating a need to consider the complete set of children's data in its entirety, and relationships among its themes, even when focusing on planning around any particular theme.

Scientific evidence about neuroscience and young children's brain development confirms that children's engagement in nurturing relationships is essential for effective brain development. Nurturing relationships and rich experiences increase the chance of children having good health, being happy, productive and creative (Perry, 2002).

The strength and quality of children's relationship with their parents and close family, relations and friends, are considered fundamental to the effective development of children's brain architecture, functions and capacity. Parenting practices such as reading to children, using complex language, responsiveness and warmth in interactions are all associated with better developmental outcomes. Conversely, a lack of positive relationships, inadequate supervision of, and involvement with, children are strongly associated with children's increased risk for behavioural and emotional problems.

Activities and play

Children identified play and specific activities as valuable in their lives. These experiences were wide-ranging and included various sports, music, dancing, crafts, attending public events and playing on playgrounds and in parks. Most noticeable was the strong relationship this theme had to the themes of the environment and family, friends and people. Activities and playing were highly important not only because of the enjoyment and novelty they provide, but also because of the time spent undertaking these activities with family and friends.

Most of the activities and play that children identified related to the environment, mainly the natural environment. A very small number of young children identified television or computer games or physical toys as important, with a preference instead for being outdoors in nature and being active with other people (running, climbing and jumping, for example). On the few occasions that televisions and computer games were identified, these were by the older children participating in the consultations.

The importance of activities and playing on children's development is identified by the UK Children's Play Council's *New Charter for Children's Play* (1998, p. 5):

> Play is an essential part of every child's life and vital to their development. It is the way children explore the world around them and develop and practice skills. It is essential for physical, emotional and spiritual growth, for intellectual and educational development, and for acquiring social and behavioural skills.

Playing and physical activity are also important for health. The Australian Healthy Eating and Physical Activity Guidelines for Early Childhood Settings (2009, p. 51) state that:

> Playing and being physically active is an important part of life for all children. The early development of good habits may lead to healthy behaviours that will last into later years, and regular physical activity in early childhood can

impact on immediate and long-term health outcomes. What's more, most children find it fun to play and be physically active!

Animals and creatures

The fourth theme that emerged as a very strong theme from all of the consultations was animals and creatures. This theme included animals in the natural environment and pets. In some instances, animals and creatures connected with the beauty and value that children ascribed to the natural environment. In other instances, this theme was about going places such as the zoo to see animals (so also about the activity itself and spending time with family). A significant number of children identified the importance of nurturing and caring for animals, the companionship provided by animals and the enjoyment of playing with pets.

Research suggests that animals have a positive influence on the development of children, physically, emotionally, socially and cognitively. Animals and pets have been found to motivate children's learning, improve relationships, foster respect for all living creatures, teach children about animals' development and help to build a sense of empathy (Melson, 2003).

Food

The fifth theme that children regularly talked about was food. In most instances, however, this theme concerned not the food itself, but rather spending time with family or going somewhere special to eat. When children talked about food that was unhealthy, they identified it as a treat. They showed a sense that such food was not the best thing to be eating on a regular basis. What was interesting in this theme is that children from a very young age showed an understanding of nutrition and what food is and is not good for them. A number of children expressed enjoying healthy food such as fruit more than sweets. Some children also expressed enjoyment of or a desire to cook for others.

Good nutrition is important in supporting the rapid growth and development that occurs during childhood. While parents largely determine young children's diets, children take greater responsibility for their own food choices as they grow older. It is therefore important to establish healthy eating patterns at young ages (Australian Institute of Health and Welfare, 2009).

Although the consultations revealed that a large number of young children have an understanding of healthy foods, research indicates that further progress is still required in Australia. The 2007 National Children's Nutrition and Physical Activity Survey found that over 60 per cent of children aged 4–8 years met the recommended daily serves of fruit (excluding juice); and only a very small proportion of children aged 4–8 years (3 per cent) met the recommended daily serves of vegetables (excluding potatoes).

Since the 2007 National Children's Nutrition and Physical Activity Survey, the Australian Healthy Eating and Physical Activity Guidelines for Early Childhood

Settings (2009) have been developed by child health and early childhood professionals in collaboration with the Australian Government Department of Health and Ageing. The 'Get Up and Grow' resources are designed to be used in a wide range of early childhood settings by families, staff and carers, and to support a consistent, national approach to childhood nutrition and physical activity.

Emotions and feelings

Emotions were identified as a theme because when children were communicating what was important to them, they often attached an emotion to it. For example, a child said, 'I like sleeping over at Grandma's house because it makes me feel safe.' Because of the number of responses that included emotional attachments, emotions and feelings was considered to be an important theme. This also reflected the fact that children's responses were well considered; they reflected on how they felt about something rather than talking about the first thing that came into their head or what they thought the adults wanted to hear. Children instead considered, 'What does this mean to me? and 'How do I feel about it?' Such consideration showed adults engaging with children in these consultations that children realised that what they were saying was important, and adults were seeing what children said as meaningful.

Interestingly, it became clear from the consultations that emotions adults would generally like to protect children from can sometimes be emotions children enjoy to experience. Notably, a large number of children identified that being scared in a controlled situation in which they felt safe (such as through play and imagination) is a highly enjoyable and sought out feeling.

Sandseter (2009, p. 94) identifies the importance on children's development of children taking risk, being challenged and being scared (which she categorises as 'exhilaration' rather than 'pure fear') in the context of play:

> the opportunity children have to take risks is an essential part of the ongoing process of 'becoming at home in the world'. The rehearsal of handling real-life risky situations through risky play is thus an important issue. It is part of children's nature to be curious about themselves and their surroundings, to discover what is safe and what is not, to try out risky activities and through this improve their perception of risk and their mastery of risky situations.

Transport

Transport was another theme that emerged in the children's data, with some children seeing travelling on the bus or in a car as something of an adventure. Often children described such travel in terms of going somewhere special so going on a train, a bus or in the car meant an enjoyable activity or experience.

Some children saw distance as a barrier to going to places they liked. Comments like, 'I don't get to go there often because it is too far away', indicated that children in the project did not always have access to transport to get them to places they may want to go. Thus most of these children's time was spent in their local community at nearby services or spaces. As the age ranges of the children consulted suggests they are too young to travel without adults present, it could be that accessibility to transport by their parents and carers may be a factor in the frequency of accessing places that young children enjoy so this could have implications for planning and better access to transport.

A 2007 report by the Victorian Council of Social Service (Fritze, 2007) identifies a number of policy and planning factors that could make public transport more suitable to parents with young children. These include: the design of public transport vehicles, buildings and facilities; accessible transport infrastructure (such as transport that is stroller/pusher friendly); continued expansion of public transport hours of operation and service frequencies on weekends and in the evenings; development of policies to increase the usability of transport services for carers of young children including: publication of when accessible bus and tram services are timetabled; removal of bus operating policies that require prams to be folded; more assistance from drivers to assist adults with prams or small children; more involvement of drivers in ensuring that adults with young children have access to priority seating; investigation of options for carrying child restraints in the taxi fleet; new planning guidelines for toilet facilities at stations and on long-distance trains to accommodate the needs of mums travelling alone with young children, including space for prams and places to safely seat young children; and increased provision of wider 'baby' car spaces at key destinations such as shopping centres.

There are, however, other possible interpretations, such as a child's perception of adequate frequency of travelling to places they enjoy, or a sense of work/life imbalance for the adults in their life that then impacts on their available time to travel to distant places as a family. Any planning in relation to transport and young children would require further investigation as to the underlying factors impacting on the frequency of young children's travel.

The future

The future was identified as another theme as children often talked about what they would like to do when they grow up. Sometimes it would be things that they saw their older siblings doing. Some children talked about liking to cook but that there was not a 'child-sized kitchen' available. Comments such as this led the researchers to ask questions such as: 'Why can't they do that now? It's very possible to build a child-sized kitchen.' This thinking about what children wish for in the future identified the kinds of things that could be possible and taken into account in community planning.

As stated by Atance and Meltzoff (2005, p. 341):

thinking about the future is an integral aspect of human cognition. Much of our behaviour is future-oriented. For instance, in choosing a career path, we may anticipate how the various options will contribute to our future happiness and success. We then modify our present actions to bring about these future goals.

In any community planning, it is relevant to consider activities young children would like to participate in when they are older and question why an age appropriate alternative of the activity is not available to enable children to participate from a younger age. For example, one child identified that the slippery slide at their local park is too big for them to use until they grow bigger. Identifying this problem in a particular community assists planning for any future upgrades of the play equipment at that park or surrounding locations.

Participation

The importance of communication was only directly identified by young children a small number of times in the context of wanting to be able to participate and be asked what their views are. However, from an observational perspective the children who volunteered to participate clearly enjoyed expressing their views and appreciated that adults were listening really well to them – as we saw illustrated time and again in the previous case study chapters.

There appeared to be a strong sense of wanting to participate and be heard. The theme of participation was also highly important for the large number of children with additional needs participating, many of which expressed themselves through non-verbal means such as digital cameras and step-by-step communicators.

Involving young children in community decision-making is not only important for the development of children and for ensuring more relevant planning around children's activities, facilities and services, it also develops a community centred philosophy in children from a young age which results in a greater likelihood of participation in their communities as adults, with immeasurable social and economic benefits to all.

The consultations undertaken with young children demonstrated that all children, regardless of age or capabilities, are able to express their views and preferences through various means of communication. Often it is not the inability of a child to express themselves effectively that is in question but rather the willingness of an adult to take the time to listen and understand that child.

Uptake of children's messages from the consultations

The journey from the idea of including young children in a government's statewide community consultation to reporting the outcomes of these conversations with

128 Reporting and uptake of children's messages

children was a long one, travelled with due diligence and care. But beyond those immediately involved, did the consultations mean anything? If they did, what did they mean?

What happens next is as important as all that has gone before. Providing feedback to children and all who were involved in the consultations, tracking uptake and communicating to stakeholders and the broader community, are all key elements of these final stages of meaningful consultations with children.

Tracking uptake of children's messages and reporting on these publicly provided a mechanism of accountability against the Children's Voices Project's intended purpose, and provided an incentive for action to be taken. Tracking uptake also provided a means for giving feedback to children and educators involved in the consultations – thereby demonstrating that the process was not a tokenistic exercise and that children's expression of views and opportunity to influence change in the community are their fundamental rights as citizens in our democratic society.

Opportunities were taken to share the outcomes of children's consultations with the wider community through media, professional journals and organisational networks, to promote the importance of the undertaking. Doing so demonstrated further afield the value of children's voices and influences in the community, and may promote similar practices elsewhere.

When asked to describe ways in which information from children's consultations informed the review of the state's strategic plan, the Manager of Community Engagement and Consultations for the State Strategic Plan replied that the consultations 'directly informed' the review:

> This was about hearing what the public thought [the state's key] aspirations should be. So based on everything we heard, we were able to distill that down a few aspiration statements there are in the new plan . . . It's literally what people told us that appears as priorities for this state.

Facilitating DPC's uptake of children's messages was the perceived clarity of the DECS Report that contained core themes as well as children's own words:

> The way we got the information from DECS was really clear. I mean, it was still in children's own words, and it's still their ideas, but it was really clear. We didn't then have to spend time trying to understand or reinterpret what was written . . . I use the words, 'the honesty of the process' . . . We were very lucky that DECS did a lot of work in terms of making sure that the way they reported [children's messages] was very clear. So that when we received the report, we were able to instantly go, 'Oh well that's all about the environment' or 'That's clearly about parks and public space'.

As an outcome of children's participation, their views were represented in the Community Engagement Board's report to the government with recommended

Reporting and uptake of children's messages 129

updates to the South Australian Strategic Plan. The Community Engagement Board (CEB) was appointed by the state's premier to oversee the entire statewide consultation process across age groups, communities and regions.

The CEB Report made a number of recommendations with regard to children and addresses almost all of the themes identified by young children in consultations either with children specifically or larger community groups that were inclusive of children. The 'ultimate target' proposed for the updated SA Strategic Plan was 'the wellbeing of our children, our families and people in our communities, now and in the future'.

How the nine themes that emerged from children's consultations aligned with the CEB Report's recommendations to the government, is discussed below in relation to each theme. We do so by revisiting briefly each theme discussed in detail earlier in this chapter, and then providing an overview of how these themes were taken up in the report's recommendations.

The *natural environment*, one of the strongest themes identified by children, expressing a sense of connection with nature and wanting to preserve and look after the natural environment, was included as one of the new priorities recognised in the report and became one of the seven new 'visions' proposed.

The value children ascribed to the *built environment*, wishing for more enjoyable places to explore in their communities – and in particular, more engaging and better designed spaces – aligned with the CEB Report's recommended new goal related to 'people friendly open spaces' and in particular identified 'the need for safe and interactive environments for children, such as parks and playgrounds, and child-friendly urban design' (Community Engagement Board, 2011, p. 67).

Throughout the consultations, young children consistently identified the importance of spending time with *family, friends and people*. The CEB Report likewise recognised as a new priority 'the importance of family, and of having strong families' (Community Engagement Board, 2011, p. 21). This report emphasised the important roles that families play in children's lives and the importance of communities supporting families and children, which will in turn assist communities to thrive. The importance of families spending more quality time together in terms of work/life balance for parents was also identified.

Children throughout the consultations identified the importance of *playing and undertaking activities*. This theme related to both spending more time sharing activities with loved ones, and having more vibrant and engaging spaces to explore. In addition to 'child-friendly urban design' and families having more time to spend with children, the CEB Report recognised as one of the seven proposed visions a need for our communities to be 'vibrant places to live, work, play and visit' (Community Engagement Board, 2011, p. 66).

Children identified the importance of *animals* in their natural environments, nurturing relationships with pets, and sharing experiences with families such as visiting the zoo. It would be a stretch to say that animals were specifically identified in the CEB Report. However, fundamental reasons behind children

130 Reporting and uptake of children's messages

identifying animals – for example, the beauty of animals in nature or having more time to spend with their families in activities that involve animals such as visiting the zoo – are all elements that were addressed in terms of the CEB Report's recommendations under the first three themes discussed above – that is, protecting the environment, more time with family and undertaking activities.

Young children valued *food* in terms of cooking and going places with family and friends to eat. Although identifying junk or unhealthy food, young children identified these as a 'treat' with a good understanding of the importance of healthy eating. One of the new priorities identified in the CEB Report also related to food, in terms of 'buying local food, growing our own food at home and protecting our food-growing land' (Community Engagement Board, 2011, p. 21).

Young children spoke of their *emotions* – in particular, feeling happy and safe. The CEB Report also recognized the importance of emotions, with its vision of wellbeing foregrounded in terms of 'feeling and being safe'. As a key recommendation, the CEB Report recommended that a 'wellbeing index' be developed at the state or national level, a valuable tool in linking emotions and wellbeing.

A large number of young children identified the importance of *transport*, particularly public transport in accessing places and activities they enjoy. A significant number of children identified that places they enjoy visiting were simply not accessible due to a lack of a family car or public transport to those places. The CEB Report proposed a vision of being 'connected to our communities' (Community Engagement Board, 2011, p. 38), with improved transport as a key focus. Access to spaces and transport are identified in a number of new goals throughout the report, particularly with regards to the importance of urban design in accessing spaces and in terms of public transport.

Young children frequently identified *the future* and possibilities for changes for a better future throughout the consultations. Likewise, the CEB Report identified that all community participants (adults and children alike) 'reflected that they want the best possible future. That future will see people enjoy a good life and be free from financial hardship, and where the environment that sustains our prosperity is protected' (Community Engagement Board, 2011, p. 73). The SA Strategic Plan itself is, of course, a plan for South Australia's future, reflecting that the importance that children placed on the future was shared at the statewide level through the plan itself.

The consultations with young children demonstrated the desire of young children for *participation* in decisions and having their voices heard. This was particularly important for very young children who were unable to articulate their desires through speech alone, the large number of non-verbal children that participated, linguistically diverse children and children in remote locations. Under the vision of being 'connected to our communities', the CEB Report identified the importance of improved communication, and recommended that the government adopt: principles and guidelines for effective community consultations; new communication channels (particularly through improved technology); and continued ongoing consultations to inform policy development, service delivery and decision-making.

It is interesting to note that Australia's *Early Years Learning Framework*'s focus on children's sense of belonging, being and becoming is reflected in the CEB Report's goal for the wider community, children and adults alike: 'We have a sense of place, identity, belonging and purpose' (Community Engagement Board, 2011, p. 39), reflecting a similar set of values for the whole community.

Valuing children's participation through feedback

In any respectful relationship in which individuals are asked to participate and express their views, they should be fully informed of the outcomes of their input. This is as important for adults as it is for children and demonstrates that children's input has been valued and that the relationship is that of a partnership – and provides a sense of closure to the project for all who were involved (Mason, 2009).

Outcomes of the consultations with young children were communicated with children to provide them with an understanding of the changes across society they helped to influence. This feedback was provided to the children's services staff facilitating the consultations to share with the children and included: a summary report of the views of children from across the state; a summary of the aspects of children's views that were incorporated into the update of the State Strategic Plan; and information about the research aligned with the project which will empower state and local government agencies to continue to value children's input into decision-making and policies across various settings.

There also was a special gallery exhibition open to the public in the foyer of the downtown DECS building. This exhibition, as shown in Figure 9.1, contained children's artworks from the consultations across the state, with children and their families encouraged to attend. This exhibition provided an important sense of closure to the Children's Voices Project – and, as importantly, a celebration of children's participation as valued, active citizens.

Action was taken to ensure children's views were included in policy and decision-making. This action extended beyond advice to the CEB with responsibility for advising the government on views of the community from across the state (as already described in detail in this chapter). An ongoing education and training programme for local government was developed and continues to be implemented across a range of local government jurisdictions. This programme disseminates children's views (especially those relevant to particular jurisdictions), and develops strategies for undertaking similar consultations in local government jurisdictions in the development of a 'social plan' for the community.

Another legacy of the Children's Voices Project has been the development of research-based tools to inform best practice in order to facilitate further consultations across the state, aligned with the government's commitment to

Figure 9.1 Exhibition of children's artworks from the Children's Voices Project

Child Friendly Cities. The tools developed to empower others to undertake meaningful children's participation drew on the learning journey made possible through the investigation of the Children's Voices Project throughout its six phases of planning, professional development, implementation, documentation, reporting and tracking uptake. It is to our reflections upon the learning journey afforded by the Children's Voices Project that we now turn, to conclude our book.

Chapter 10

Final reflections on the Children's Voices Project

Problem-posing education affirms men and women as beings in the process of becoming.

(Freire, 1983, p. 72)

The South Australian Children's Voices Project began with a simple idea, opportunistic timing, a range of challenges and with modest, yet symbolic outcomes in mind. From there, the project evolved and grew, and continues to shape the way children and young people's citizenship is viewed and enacted in South Australia, bolstered by the state government's strengthened public commitment to the UN Convention on the Rights of the Child and the UNICEF Child Friendly Cities Framework.

These consultations looked beyond child-specific issues to whole-of-community matters and provided an opportunity to frame children's participation in terms of their active citizenship instead of confining their experiences to child-specific services or settings. Consequently, the consultation theme was developed to explore with young children across the state, 'What is important to children in their communities and what do children wish for in their lives?'

The Children's Voices Project also was a symbolic undertaking to showcase to those not working in fields directly with children that children's views are highly significant and deeply valued in a democratic society. It would be one achievement to simply include children's views on this one occasion, and quite another to demonstrate the depth and influence the views of a child can have in our society.

These consultations were by educators' own admission a deeply transforming experience. The experience of meaningfully consulting with children about their local communities saw highly skilled early childhood educators re-frame their thinking and actions in exploring what it means to be fully engaged with children as agents in their own lives and learning – fully engaging with children, that is, from diverse cultural backgrounds living in high to low socio-economic circumstances in urban, suburban, rural and remote localities.

This final chapter brings together educators' key re-framings drawn from their accounts of what changed for them as a consequence of this experience – and

134 Final reflections on the Children's Voices Project

how these changes, in turn, impacted on the work of the education and child development policy officer co-ordinating the consultations. As these re-framings will show, consulting meaningfully with young children about matters important in their lives is no small feat – it requires deep thinking, careful planning, meticulous documentation, and a call to dialogue and appropriate action sustained over time *with*, not *for*, children in and with the world.

Educators' re-framings

In their encounters with children in the Children's Voices Project, educators found themselves reviewing their established thoughts and practices in light of what they found was not working or could work better; as well as what educators found worked despite themselves and their own misgivings – as we saw in the previous case study chapters. These tensions provide what have been called pivotal moments that see educators re-frame their thoughts and actions (Loughran, 2005; Loughran and Northfield, 1998; Harris, 2010). In the Children's Voices Project, these moments were central to unearthing insights into what it means to authentically encounter the child and engage with children's voices.

Educators witnessed first-hand the depth and intensity of children's involvement, seeing the world from children's perspectives. They included all children who wished to participate and enabled children's participation by clarifying and developing with them the terms and tools of engagement. This experience saw educators shift from wondering, 'Can children really do this?' to affirming, 'Look at what children can do'. In making this shift, educators saw and appreciated anew the competent child.

In the educators' remarks about children's engagement – such as remarks shared in the case study chapters and elsewhere in this book – we see educators recognising children's humanity and coming to understand more deeply what it means to be and become fully human (after Freire, 1983). Children's ongoing realisation of their ontological vocations was fostered by creating situations that allowed children's humanity to shine through and to bring this humanity to bear on their participation as citizens to inform decision-making processes. In seeing this process at work, educators more greatly realised their own identity as educators in a political sense of democracy and enabling (not hindering) democratic process and citizenship.

In enabling young children's democratic process and citizenship in and with their world, educators released control and experienced children's sense of empowerment. In so doing, educators re-framed their actions from 'doing to or for children' to 'doing with children and seeing the world through their children's eyes'. Dichotomy between educator and child was broken down as educator and child alike entered into a community of learners where children's agency was free to do its work – and where children were the subjects of their own educative encounters rather than objects of educational agendas.

Final reflections on the Children's Voices Project 135

Releasing control to the children paradoxically augmented educators' own sense of empowerment. As Brett (2007) has argued:

> The promotion of knowledge and skills for democratic participation is at the heart of citizenship education. But how are young people best taught to be 'change-makers', prepared to speak out on issues that concern them? If citizenship education is to achieve more than merely encouraging functional participation and empower young people with the skills to challenge perceived injustices, it needs to confront a widespread fatalism about the fixity of politics and society. For this to happen, teachers need to have a sense of themselves as change agents, too.

In the Children's Voices Project, educators felt empowered by the dialogic process at the heart of the consultations – as was child, so was educator, one with the other about their world. Through this dialogic process, children and educators sustained meaningful conversations with one another, which saw another significant re-framing in educators' practices – re-framing 'transient interactions with children' as 'meaningful dialogue with and among children'. In this re-framing, educators and children alike experienced what it means to enter into authentic dialogue with young children.

Children's engagement was optimised through partnerships in the community, including local artists, musicians, dramatists, dancers and choreographers. Through these partnerships, there was a broadening of approach beyond educational institutions to the wider community. These partnerships were resonant with what educators were already doing, but now educators were using these partnerships in a new way – a means for nurturing and enriching means through which children exert their agency and exercise their citizenship.

Enriching children's tools of engagement in the dialogue about their communities contributed to both the rich authenticity of educators' documentation, and the challenges arising from the complex, multi-modal nature of this work. The task of documentation in such a context provoked another re-framing among educators – re-framing 'recording observations' to 'authentic documentation' that makes the child visible and their voice heard, and is faithful to the child's words, creations and the meaning intent behind them.

A principal policy adviser reflects

The Children's Voices Project was viewed from a policy perspective to be about good community engagement practice and providing children with a voice. The experience, however, has reshaped thinking around the importance of children's consultation to be about much more than voice. The overarching consideration is children's citizenship – and children's valued, active citizenship at that.

It is clear that as a society we too often overlook children's identities as valued citizens now rather than only citizens of the future. Children may be defined narrowly in terms of their settings (such as a student), their relationship to adults (such as someone's son or daughter), their age (such as a four-year-old), as part of a homogenous group (such as a toddler), or in terms of their future potential – without recognising the richness that children's current contributions bring to the diversity and fabric of society here and now.

Our challenge as a society is to look beyond children in the family and children in a service or programme setting to recognise children as valued citizens. As a key to valued, active citizenship, ongoing opportunities need to be created to empower children and young people's voice and participation in their communities, to ensure society is reflective of their rights and responsibilities as it is for other citizens.

The word 'valued' is important, as it is not enough to simply involve children, but to listen and take seriously their views and translate them into action by influencing decision-making and the shaping of policy. There is a need to re-frame our thinking about children, even when we have their best interests at heart, to recognise that we are not experts on every child, but rather champions and advocates for children. In so doing, it is important to endeavour to work with children as partners.

Like much of society, South Australia has a long way to go to empower and recognise all children as equal citizens. It has demonstrated, however, a commitment to doing so through a range of avenues, including the development of children's plans at the local government level, and proposed child development legislation to entrench children's valued citizenship, participation and voice across local and state-wide decision-making processes.

Valuing children's citizenship is a whole-of-society responsibility that extends beyond government. Therefore, a key imperative is to advocate and create opportunities for children's participation, whether it be: facilitating children's input to improving child-specific services or programmes; ensuring children are included in consultations planned for the wider community; or creating new opportunities to consult with children on issues they have identified as important to them in their communities and seeking community action as a result.

A key strength of the Children's Voices Project was the partnership approach taken, the people involved and the synergies among them. In many cases those with the skills, expertise and established relationships to most authentically engage with children are not directly involved in public policy decisions or practices. Likewise, those with responsibility for public policy are generally not best placed to facilitate meaningful consultation processes with children. So success relied on strong connections among those engaged in the fields of research, policy and practice, while ensuring that children were at the heart of the complete encounter.

Another key strength of the Children's Voices Project was its principle-based approach, recognising that a prescribed approach would devalue the expertise that educators and children brought to the table. This principle-based approach is discussed in further detail below.

Final reflections on the Children's Voices Project   137

A principle-based framework for children's participation

A set of suggestions was developed to operationalise the principles that under-pinned the consultations as dialogic encounter in the Children's Voices Project, in recognition that to provide prescriptive or lock-step instructions would disempower children and adults alike. These suggestions were subsequently developed further, based on further reflections and evidence from the investiga-tion of the project. These principles are set out in Table 10.1 and considered in further detail below:

*   *Build mutual respect and gain consent* – In order to foster mutual respect it is important for children's participation to be voluntary and for children to be invited rather than expected to participate in the consultations. For particularly young children or where photos, audio, visual footage or artistic works are to be shared publicly, it is also necessary to obtain parental consent.
*   *Explore questions as themes* – When undertaking consultations with children, it is important to frame the questions as themes to be explored and allow adequate time for exploration of the subject matter. Young children in particular may not be able to verbally express themselves in ways older children and adults might, so direct on-the-spot questioning is not likely to engage young children and tune into their views in an authentic manner.
*   *Break down subject matter into its various elements* – Children may not have prior experience or understanding of the theme being explored, and so a

Table 10.1 Suggestions for framing consultations as dialogic encounter

Build Mutual Respect and Gain Consent	Explore Questions as Themes	Break Down Subject Matter into its Various Elements
The Process is Just as Important as the Outcome	Involve Children in the Shaping of the Consultation Process	Use Visual References or Visit Locations Being Discussed
Take Care to Capture Children's Authentic Views	Hand the Tools of Expression to the Child	Use Language that Invites Genuine Input
Use Reflective Language	Consider Messages Conveyed through Body Language	Acknowledge the Power Difference
Consider the Dynamic of Children in a Group Setting	Explore Themes in a Way that is Meaningful to Each Child's Experiences	Ascertain Children's Feelings as Well as their Views
Take the Time to Understand the Real Meaning Behind what is Being Expressed	Provide Feedback about the Value of Children's Input	Most importantly, participation by children should be voluntary, engaging, challenging and rewarding

process whereby children are able to develop an understanding and a view on a particular matter is a key to a consultation process in which children's authentic voices are heard. The subject matter should be broken down into its various elements to be explored to ensure a deeper understanding of the issues.

- *The process is just as important as the outcome* – It is important to recognise that the consultation process is just as significant as the information received. All children should feel valued and their views listened to; and feel they are sharing their views in a safe and secure situation where those around them have a genuine interest in what they say and do.
- *Involve children in shaping the consultation process* – Provide information to children as to how and why they are being invited to express their views and provide the opportunity for them to shape the consultations in a way they would find most engaging and enjoyable. Doing so helps to develop shared understandings among children and adults as to the purpose of the consultations; and gives children a voice in shaping how the consultations occur.
- *Use visual references or visit locations being discussed* – Showing photos of your community taken from the eye level of a child may be a good visual reference for children. A walk or drive around the community to discuss local landmarks, places and spaces is also recommended.
- *Take care to capture children's authentic views* – Digitally record or write down what children say verbatim, in large print exactly as they say it to ensure we don't put adult spin on their words. In doing so, we need to be careful that this scribing is not intrusive and that adults can keep up with what children say without breaking the flow of children's ideas.
- *Hand the tools of expression to the child* – Support and enable children to express their views by asking lead questions, providing concrete stimuli (e.g. photos), and handing the tools for expression to the child. These 'tools' might be a camera, paints or crayons, or having the floor to have their say. Scaffold children's views by extending and re-formulating what they say to check for shared understanding and more fully draw out what they are expressing; and prompt them to elaborate where they can.
- *Use language that invites genuine input* – Show you are handing the agenda to the child by expressions such as: 'Tell me, what do you think about . . .?'; 'How do you feel about . . .?'; 'What do you like about . . .?'; 'What makes you think that?'; 'What makes you feel that way?' These kinds of questions explicitly seek to project children into the dialogue that ensues.
- *Use reflective language* – Use reflective language in your conversations with children – for example, 'I see you have taken lots of outdoor photos. Is that because you like doing things outside?'
- *Consider messages conveyed through body language* – Tune into children's body language – not just what they say but how they say it. Attend to their tone, facial expressions, gestures, gaze and so on.

Final reflections on the Children's Voices Project 139

- *Acknowledge the power difference* – Acknowledge the power difference between children and adults. Are the children expressing how they feel or what they think adults want to hear?
- *Consider the dynamic of children in a group setting* – Also acknowledge the dynamic among children when engaging in group discussions and activities. Are some children dominating while others sit quietly on the sidelines? Are children saying what they think or seem to be just agreeing with what their peers are saying? Are all children being given opportunity to express what it is they mean?
- *Explore themes in a way that is meaningful to each child's experiences* – It may be best to ask children what they like to do or would like to do in their communities rather than what facilities or services they would like. Be as concrete and specific as possible about the questions and prompts you use to engage children's views. Other examples include asking about places children like going to and any favourite places they might have; people they like seeing, talking with, playing with, spending time with, and where.
- *Ascertain children's feelings as well as their views* – Bear in mind, too, that these consultations also seek to find out what children might not like in their communities, so provide opportunities to find out about the 'downside' too, in specific and concrete terms as above.
- *Take the time to understand the real meaning behind what is being expressed* – If drawings are used as an artistic medium for children expressing their views then always ask for more detail on what a child has drawn. It is important not to assume we understand what has been drawn, why it has been drawn or what it represents. Children often talk as they draw, even if just to themselves, and express themselves non-verbally (such as scribbling or drawing very quickly). Tune in to the comments children make as they draw and the gestures they make, and note these down carefully for later reference to enrich records of what children conveyed.
- *Provide feedback about the value of children's input* – Provide feedback to children about what will happen after their participation in the consultation strategies and how their views have been important in helping to shape their communities. To do so shows that their views are valued and respected.

Of course as an overarching consideration, most importantly, participation by children should be voluntary, engaging, challenging and rewarding.

Concluding reflections

Consulting with young children as part of a statewide initiative was based on a genuine respect for children's rights and an authentic need to find out what they think. The consultations were much more than a tokenistic gesture – they provided for meaningful engagement and a provocation for re-framing what we think and do as adults engaged in early childhood business.

In the context here of engaging with young children's voices to learn their views of their communities and lives, the word 'consultation' is a misnomer – it belies the depth and complexity of this engagement. On the one hand, 'consultation' is appropriate as two of its definitions are meeting with an expert and referring to a source of information. Clearly, in the Children's Voices Project, children were both experts and critical sources of information. But the word 'consultation' can also carry unfortunate connotations of tokenistic or lip-service gestures to be seen to be doing something rather than doing something meaningfully. Clearly what happened in this space not tokenistic.

Rather, it was a genuine encounter based on an unequivocal belief in children's capacity for dialogue. This capacity was realised through the Children's Voices Project's approach to the consultations through play and multi-modal experiences. Children were given opportunity to further develop and enrich their tools for engaging in the consultations – tools transferable to other aspects of children's lives. Children, too, were supported by a process of co-construction with educators in and about their world. This co-construction balanced children's agency and dependency, and clarified and developed shared understandings about the terms of engagement.

Children's participation was endowed with authenticity and meaning, with every effort made to shape the encounter with the children; document the process and outcomes in ways that were true to children's voices; and honour the purpose of the consultations by being transparent and accountable.

The consultations were framed as dialogic encounter, infused with hope for what could transpire from the consultations; faith of participants in the government's intention to pay heed; children's love for their world and those in it; mutual trust among participants in one another's competence and that the encounter would be worthwhile and have consequence; humility in recognising young children's competence; and thinking that perceives reality in transformation, and children re-imagining reality through their actions in and projections onto the world.

In this encounter, then, we saw a (further) awakening of children's consciousness as citizens, and adults' conscientisation of children as active competent citizens with voices to be heard.

The dialogue needs to be continued with children – how, for example, might children be part of the solutions to the problems they identified or wishes they sought to be fulfilled and, in getting to the heart of the experience itself, what did children's participation mean to them?

Were these consultations successful? By all accounts above, and rewards that have since ensued, the answer appears to be an unequivocal 'yes'. The recurring messages from sites and the two government agencies is that tuning into children's voices in authentic ways and for real purposes is highly worthwhile, deeply challenging, and transformative for those directly consulting with children and those who take up the information gathered from these consultations to inform strategic state planning.

Final reflections on the Children's Voices Project   141

There can be no doubt, on the strength of the evidence presented in this book, that the consultations had transformative outcomes for all involved – children in the sense that they were being asked genuine questions about what mattered to them, given ample opportunity and time for sustained engagement in these interactions, and validated as citizens in a democratic society; educators in re-framing their thoughts and actions and developing new insights and fresh practices; DECS in terms of entering into genuine relationships of collaboration and learning from what young children reveal and seeing what worked and what might be improved in eliciting young children's voices; DPC in terms of moving from some initial uncertainty about the ability and feasibility of engaging young children's voices to seeing the worthwhile and valid contributions that children make.

What would be of further research interest, however, is to document children's own reflections on their consultation experiences. It was not possible to do so for these consultations, but it would be highly worthwhile doing in future research of such initiatives. DECS personnel included children's own words in their final report, and a mapping of the community engagement report clearly showed the inclusion of children's messages. What did not appear, however, were explicit links to what young children said. The ability to differentiate what young children expressed will be critical to the success of what is to come next – the operationalisation of the government's political priorities around developing a child-friendly state.

This consultation initiative did not set out to transform early childhood practices but rather to draw on educators' expertise in implementing the consultations with young children. While this expertise in no small way contributed to the perceived success of the consultations, educators' involvement also saw re-framing of their thinking and transformation of their practices. The extent to which these changes would endure or have indeed endured since the project's end is unknown – and worthy of further research. This is not to say that the processes involved in preparing, planning, implementing, documenting, interpreting and collating these consultations were perfect – they were not, and many lessons are to be learned about what worked and what could be improved, as noted throughout this chapter.

Questions raised as to how these practices might be sustained in the systems in which they work are beginning to be addressed. Consultations undertaken with young children for the purposes of informing South Australia's Strategic Plan were not an isolated exercise. There are already further consultations underway or in development with a range of partners and for a range of purposes including: the development of Children's Plans with local government; action research by students in various fields including early childhood, physiotherapy and occupational therapy; consultations to inform programme reviews by organisations delivering services for children and families; consultations to inform the design of child friendly environments and consultations to inform Australian Early Development Index (AEDI) planning as some examples. It is becoming more

142 Final reflections on the Children's Voices Project

visible that the only effective and meaningful way to build communities *for* children is to build communities in partnership *with* children while recognising that a society that values and respects its children is a society that values and respects all of its citizens from childhood through to adulthood.

Professional development opportunities have also been offered and will continue in partnership with the researcher (Harris) involved in this project. A Gowrie and Early Childhood Australia session for educators as well as forums for local government personnel through the Local Government Association, including architects and town planners are just a couple of examples of the diversity of audiences that have shown interest in children's participation among a large number of forums that continue to be presented in order to empower others to seek children's views in a range of decision-making across the state.

Ultimately, the consultations with young children to inform the review of South Australia's Strategic Plan achieved far greater outcomes than was initially thought possible. The initial aim was to simply give children a voice among others in this particular consultation process. What resulted, however, was a demonstration of children's valued citizenship and a whole of community partnership with children, early childhood practitioners, parents, researchers and policy makers coming together to transform the view of the child from a passive recipient of nurture within society to an active and equal citizen now, not a citizen of the future. As a result there has been increased interest and undertakings by state and local governments to include children in decision-making in an authentic and meaningful way and so the learning journey of dialogic encounter continues for child and adult alike, as equal partners and co-contributors to the rich diversity of society across the age equilibrium.

To take us forward in dialogue, we consider it important to do what was not possible in the Children's Voices Project – and that is explore with children what they learned about themselves as citizens from such an encounter. Reflection is an important part of learning about citizenship and one's rights, responsibilities and actions as a citizen – and brings with it in the context of engaging with young children the genesis of political literacy. An age-old proverb states:

> Tell me, I forget;
> Show me, I remember;
> Involve me, I understand.

To this proverb and in the spirit of the principles framing this book, we add our own fourth line:

> Empower me, I thrive.

Through empowerment, we are able to reflect and act on what we understand, and so continue to grow and become more fully human.

References

Alderson, P., Hawthorne, J. and Killen, M. (2005) The participation rights of premature babies. *International Journal of Children's Rights*, 13: 31–50.

Atance, C. M. and Meltzoff, A. N. (2005) *My future self: young children's ability to anticipate and explain future states.* University of Washington, Institute for Learning and Brain Sciences, USA.

Australian Government Department of Education, Employment and Workplace Relations (DEEWR) (2009) *Belonging, being and becoming: the early years learning framework for Australia.* Commonwealth of Australia, Canberra.

Australian Government Department of Education, Employment and Workplace Relations (DEEWR) (2011) *My time, our place.* Commonwealth of Australia, Canberra. http://deewr.gov.au/my-time-our-place-framework-school-age-care-australia (retrieved 15 June 2013).

Australian Government Department of Health and Ageing (2009) *Get up and grow: healthy eating and physical activity for early childhood* (Family Book).

Australian Institute of Health and Welfare (2009) *A picture of Australia's children 2009.* Cat. No. PHE 112. Canberra: AIHW.

Ben-Arieh, A. and Boyer, Y. (2005) Citizenship and childhood: the state of affairs in Israel. *Childhood*, 12(1): 33–53.

Bishop, K. (2009) Participating in research: what's it really like for kids? In *Involving children and young people in research [electronic resource]: a compendium of papers and reflections from a think tank co-hosted by the Australian Research Alliance for Children and Youth and the NSW Commission for Children and Young People on 11 November 2008*, pp. 28–37. http://www.childhealthresearch.org.au/media/54379/involvingchildrenandyoungpeopleinresearch_1_.pdf (retrieved 26 June 2013).

Brett, P. (2007) Endowing participation with meaning: citizenship education, Paolo Freire and educating young people as change-makers. http://www.citized.info/pdf/commarticles/Endowing%20Participation%20Peter%20Brett.pdf (retrieved 17 May 2013).

Children's Play Council (1998) *The new charter for children's play.* London.

Clark, A., Kjorholt, A. T. and Moss, P. (eds) (2005) *Beyond listening: children's perspectives on early childhood services.* Bristol, UK: The Policy Press.

Coady, M. (2008) Beings and becomings: historical and philosophical considerations of the child as citizen. In Mac Naughton, G., Hughes, P. and Smith, K. (eds) *Young children as active citizens.* Cambridge Scholars Publishing: Newcastle, pp. 2–14.

144 References

Community Engagement Board (2011) *South Australia's plan for the best: 2020 and beyond*. Adelaide.http://www.google.com.au/?gws_rd=cr#bav=on.2,or.r_qf.&fp=dfac927e2fd30f7a&q=South+Australia's+Plan+for+the+best:+2020+and+beyond (retrieved 1 June 2013).

Corbin, J. and Strauss, A. (2008) *Basics of qualitative research: techniques and procedures for developing grounded theory (3rd edn)*. Thousand Oaks, CA: Sage.

Council of Australian Governments (2009) *Investing in the early years – a national early childhood development strategy*. Commonwealth of Australia, Canberra.

Council of Europe (2011) *Consultation on the draft Council of Europe Strategy on the Rights of the Child*, Strasbourg.

Delpit, L. (2003) Educators as 'seed people' growing a new future. *Educational Researcher*, 32(7): 14–21.

Dockett, S. (2009) Engaging young children in research. In *Involving children and young people in research [electronic resource]: a compendium of papers and reflections from a think tank co-hosted by the Australian Research Alliance for Children and Youth and the NSW Commission for Children and Young People on 11 November 2008*, pp. 52–63. http://www.childhealthresearch.org.au/media/54379/involving childrenandyoungpeopleinresearch_1_.pdf (retrieved 26 June 2013).

Edwards, C., Gandini, L. and Forman, G. (eds) (2012) *The hundred languages of children: the Reggio Emilia experience in transformation (3rd edn)*. Westport, Connecticut: Ablex Publishing.

Fitzgerald, R. and Graham, A. (2009) 'Young people big voice': reflections on the participation of children and young people in a university setting. In *Involving children and young people in research [electronic resource]: a compendium of papers and reflections from a think tank co-hosted by the Australian Research Alliance for Children and Youth and the NSW Commission for Children and Young People on 11 November 2008*, pp. 64–75. http://www.childhealthresearch.org.au/media/54379/involvingchildrenandyoungpeopleinresearch_1_.pdf (retrieved 26 June 2013).

Freire, P. (1983) *Pedagogy of the oppressed*. Continuum, New York.

Freire, P. and Frei Betto (1985) *The politics of education: culture, power and liberation*. Bergin & Garvey: Amhurst.

Fritze, J. (2007) *Young mums and transport in Victoria: 'You might as well just stay at home'*. Melbourne: Victorian Council of Social Service.

Glesne, C. (2006) *Becoming qualitative researchers: an introduction*, Boston, MA: Pearson.

Hallett, C. and Prout, A. (eds) (2003) *Hearing the voices of children: social policy for a new century*. Routledge Falmer: London.

Harcourt, D. (2009) Standpoints on quality: young children as competent research participants. In *Involving children and young people in research [electronic resource]: a compendium of papers and reflections from a think tank co-hosted by the Australian Research Alliance for Children and Youth and the NSW Commission for Children and Young People on 11 November 2008*, pp. 76–88. http://www.childhealthresearch.org.au/media/54379/involvingchildrenandyoungpeopleinresearch_1_.pdf (retrieved 26 June 2013).

Harris, P. (2009) *Language learning in the baby and toddler years*. Terrigal, NSW: David Barlow Publishing.

References 145

——(2010) Mediating relationships between research, policy and practice in a professional development context. *Studying Teacher Education*, 6(1): 75–94.

Hart, Roger A. (1992) *Children's participation: from tokenism to citizenship*. UNICEF International Child Development Centre (now Innocenti Research Centre), Florence.

Heckman, J. J. and Masterov, D. V. (2007) The productivity argument for investing in young children. *Review of Agricultural Economics*, 29(3): 446–93.

Hobsons Bay City Council (2009) *Children's plan 2009–2013: community consultation report June 2009*, Victoria.

Invernizzi, A. and Williams, J. (2008) *Children and citizenship*. London: Sage.

Kelly, L., Main, S., Dockett, S., Perry, B. and Heinrich, S. (2006) Listening to young children's voices in museum spaces. *Conference of the Australian Association for Research in Education*, November 2006, Adelaide.

Lansdown, G. (2005) Can you hear me? The right of young children to participate in decisions affecting them. *Working Paper 36*. Bernard van Leer Foundation, The Hague.

Lawson, N. (2005) What lessons does the pedagogical approach of Paulo Freire have for the development of citizenship as a national curriculum subject?http://www.citized.info/?strand=2&r_menu=sr (retrieved 18 June 2013).

Loughran, J. (2005) Researching teaching about teaching: self-study of teacher education practices. *Studying Teacher Education*, 1(1): 5–16.

Loughran, J. and Northfield, J. R. (1998) A framework for the development of self-study practice. In M. L. Hamilton (ed.) *Reconceptualizing teaching practice: self-study in teacher education*. London: Falmer Press, pp. 7–18.

Mac Naughton, G., Smith, K. and Lawrence, H. (2004) Hearing young children's voices. *ACT children's strategy: consulting with children birth to eight years of age*. Centre for Equity and Innovation in Early Childhood, Faculty of Education, University of Melbourne.

Mac Naughton, G., Hughes, P. and Smith, K. (eds) (2008) *Young children as active citizens*. Newcastle: Cambridge Scholars Publishing.

Makin, L., Diaz Jones, C. and McLachlan, C. (eds) (2007) *Literacies in childhood*. Sydney: Elsevier.

Mason, J. (2009) Strategies and issues in including children as participants in research on children's needs in care: a case study. In *Involving children and young people in research [electronic resource]: a compendium of papers and reflections from a think tank co-hosted by the Australian Research Alliance for Children and Youth and the NSW Commission for Children and Young People on 11 November 2008*, pp. 89–98. http://www.childhealthresearch.org.au/media/54379/involvingchildrenandyoungpeopleinresearch_1_.pdf (retrieved 26 June 2013).

Melson, G. F. (2003) Child development and the human-companion animal bond. *American Behavioural Scientist*, 47(1): 31–9.

Moloney, L. (2005) Children's voices: Reflections on the telling and the listening. *Journal of Family Studies*, 11(2): 216–26.

Moore, T., McArthur, M. and Noble-Carr, D. (2009) Taking little steps: research with children – a case study. In *Involving children and young people in research [electronic resource]: a compendium of papers and reflections from a think tank co-hosted by the Australian Research Alliance for Children and Youth and the NSW*

146 References

Commission for Children and Young People on 11 November 2008, pp. 99–110. http://www.childhealthresearch.org.au/media/54379/involvingchildrenandyou ngpeopleinresearch_1_.pdf (retrieved 26 June 2013).

Mustard, J. F. (2007) *Investing in the early years: closing the gap between what we know and what we do.* Adelaide: South Australia Department of the Premier and Cabinet.

National Children's and Youth Law Centre/UNICEF Australia (2011) *Listen to children: 2011 child right's NGO report.*

Noble-Carr, D. (2006) *Engaging children in research on sensitive issues.* A literature review for the Institute of Child Protection Studies, ACU National for the ACT Department of Disability, Housing and Community Services, Dickson, ACT. http://www.dhcs.act.gov.au/__data/assets/pdf_file/0005/10301/Engaging_ ChildrenLitReview.pdf (retrieved 21 February 2012).

Nutbrown, C. and Clough, P. (2009) Citizenship and inclusion in the early years: understanding and responding to children's perspectives of 'belonging'. *International Journal of Early Years Education*, 17(3): 191–206.

Painter, C. (1991) *Learning the mother tongue, 2nd edn.* Geelong: Deakin University Press.

Percy-Smith, B. (2010) Councils, consultations and community: rethinking the spaces for children and young people's participation. *Children's Geographies*, 8(2): 107–22.

Percy-Smith, B. and Thomas, N. (eds) (2009) *A handbook of children and young people's participation: perspectives, theory and practice.* London: Routledge.

Perry, B. (2002) Childhood experience and the expression of genetic potential: what childhood neglect tells us about nature and nurture. *In Brain and Mind*, 3: 79–100.

Phillips, L. (2011) Possibilities and quandaries for young children's active citizenship. *Early Education and Development*, 22(5): 778–94.

Prout, A. (2000) Children's participation: control and self-realisation in British late modernity. *Children and Society*, 14: 304–15.

Rhedding-Jones, J., Bae, B. and Winger, N. (2008) Young children and voice. In Mac Naughton, G., Hughes, P. and Smith, K. (eds) *Young children as active citizens.* Newcastle, UK: Cambridge Scholars Publishing, pp. 44–59.

Rinaldi, C. (2006). *In dialogue with Reggio Emilia: listening, researching and learning.* London: Routledge.

Rogoff, B. (1990) *Apprenticeship in thinking: cognitive development in social context.* New York: Oxford University Press.

Rose, J. and Rosenow, N. (2007) Positive strategies for children with sensory integration challenges. *Child Care Exchange*: September/October, 40–4.

Sandseter, E. B. H. (2009) Children's expressions of exhilaration and fear in risky play. *Contemporary Issues in Early Childhood*, 10(2): 2009.

Smith, A. B., Taylor, N. J. and Gollop, M. M. (2000) *Children's voices: research, policy and practice.* Auckland, NZ: Pearson Education New Zealand Limited.

Sommer, D., Samuelsson, I. P. and Hundeide, K. (2010) *Child perspectives and children's perspectives in theory and practice.* London: Springer.

Sorin, R. (2009) Involving young people in research in Hedland – from ideas to action: a praxis model. In *Involving children and young people in research [electronic resource]: a compendium of papers and reflections from a think tank co-hosted by the Australian Research Alliance for Children and Youth and the NSW Commission for Children and Young People on 11 November 2008*, pp. 145–55. http://www.

childhealthresearch.org.au/media/54379/involvingchildrenandyoungpeopleinres earch_1_.pdf (retrieved 26 June 2013).

Stephenson, A. (2009) Horses in the sandpit: photography, prolonged involvement and 'stepping back' as strategies for listening to children's voices. *Early Child Development and Care*, 179(2): 131–41.

Stephenson, E. (2011) Listening to young children: how conceptions of childhood affect authenticity of voice in research. Paper presented at the *Australian Association of Research in Education Conference*, Hobart, 2–6 December 2011.

Taylor, N., Smith, A. B. and Gollop, M. (2008) New Zealand children and young people's perspectives on citizenship. *International Journal of Children's Rights*, 16: 195–210.

UN Committee on the Rights of the Child (CRC) (2006) *CRC general comment no. 7 (2005): implementing child rights in early childhood*, 20 September 2006, CRC/C/GC/7/Rev.1. http://www.refworld.org/docid/460bc5a62.html (retrieved 8 August 2013).

UNICEF Innocenti Research Centre (2001) Child friendly cities. http://www.childfriendlycities.org/ (retrieved 23 February 2012).

United Nations (1989) *United Nations convention on the rights of the child*. http://www2.ohchr.org/english/law/crc.htm (retrieved 23 February 2012).

Vygotsky, L. (1978). *Mind in society: the development of higher mental processes*. Cambridge, MA: Harvard University Press.

Wise, S. (2009) Major themes and considerations. In *Involving children and young people in research [electronic resource]: a compendium of papers and reflections from a think tank co-hosted by the Australian Research Alliance for Children and Youth and the NSW Commission for Children and Young People on 11 November 2008*, pp. 168–79. http://www.childhealthresearch.org.au/media/54379/involvingchil drenandyoungpeopleinresearch_1_.pdf (retrieved 26 June 2013).

Wood, D., Bruner, J. S. and Ross, G. (1976) The role of tutoring in problem solving. *Journal of Psychology and Psychiatry*, 17: 89–100.

Woodhead, M. and Faulkner, D. (2000) Subjects, objects or participants? In Christensen, P. and James, A. (eds) *Research with children: perspectives and practices*. London and New York: Falmer Press.

Yin, R. K. (2009) *Case study research: design and methods* (4th edn). Thousand Oaks, CA: Sage Publications.

Index

children as citizens: defining 1–4; nurturing 4–9; principle–based framework for engaging 137–9

children's themes *see also* Eyre and Western Community case study; Fleurieu case study; Limestone Town case study; Western Adelaide case study

Children's Voices Project design: embedded case studies 25–8; participants 16–17; sites 17–22; procedures for gathering and analysing data 22–5; research questions 15; stages 12–13; trustworthiness 28

citizenship *see* children as citizens

dialogic encounter 6, 7, 8, 12, 15, 25–6, 29, 42, 63, 67, 68, 70, 77, 92, 100, 109, 137, 140, 142; framing purpose and problem *see* Eyre and Western Community case study; Fleurieu case study; Limestone Town case study; Western Adelaide case study; structures and modes that sustain dialogue *see* Eyre and Western Community case study; Fleurieu case study; Limestone Town case study; Western Adelaide case study

dialogue *see* dialogic encounter

documenting children's messages 106–117 *see also* Eyre and Western Community case study; Fleurieu case study; Limestone Town case study; Western Adelaide case study

educators' re-framings 3, 13, 68, 133, 134–5, 139, 141

Eyre and Western Community case study: children's themes 71–6; contextual information 65–6; documentation 109; framing purpose and problem for engagement 66–8; reflections on the case study 76–80; structures and modes that sustained dialogue 71; unfolding of the encounter 68–70

Fleurieu case study: children's themes 86–92; contextual information 81–2; documentation 109–11; framing purpose and problem for engagement 82–4; reflections on the case study 92; structures and modes that sustained dialogue 85–6; unfolding of the encounter 84–5

Limestone Town case study: children's themes 55–63; contextual information 47–8; documentation 107–8; framing purpose and problem for engagement 48–50; reflections on the case study 63–4; structures and modes that sustained dialogue 54–5; unfolding of the encounter 51–4

planning to engage with children as citizens: beyond tokenism 29–31; consultation strategies 35–6; documenting the learning journey 42–3; engaging non–traditional partners 32–3; ethical and legal matters 43–4; formulating core theme 33–5; identifying purpose 32; implementation 46; providing professional development 36–42, 44–6

reporting children's messages: children's themes 121–7; feedback 131–2; making sense of the data 119–20; reporting children's views as themes 120–1; uptake 127–31

United Nations Convention on the Rights of the Child 1, 11, 13, 34

Western Adelaide case study: children's themes 101–3; contextual information 93; documentation 111–12; framing purpose and problem for engagement 94–5; reflections on the case study 103–5; structures and modes that sustained dialogue 97–101; unfolding of the encounter 95–7

Taylor & Francis
eBooks
FOR LIBRARIES

ORDER YOUR FREE 30 DAY INSTITUTIONAL TRIAL TODAY!

Over 23,000 eBook titles in the Humanities, Social Sciences, STM and Law from some of the world's leading imprints.

Choose from a range of subject packages or create your own!

Benefits for you
- ▶ Free MARC records
- ▶ COUNTER-compliant usage statistics
- ▶ Flexible purchase and pricing options

Benefits for your user
- ▶ Off-site, anytime access via Athens or referring URL
- ▶ Print or copy pages or chapters
- ▶ Full content search
- ▶ Bookmark, highlight and annotate text
- ▶ Access to thousands of pages of quality research at the click of a button

For more information, pricing enquiries or to order a free trial, contact your local online sales team.

UK and Rest of World: **online.sales@tandf.co.uk**

US, Canada and Latin America: **e-reference@taylorandfrancis.com**

www.ebooksubscriptions.com

A flexible and dynamic resource for teaching, learning and research.